Handling data 1

NC LEVEL 4

GCSE FOUNDATION

Heinemann

Project director: Peter Reynolds
Assistant director: Mike Cornelius
Project manager: Jan Hoare

Author of this book
John Cable
Edited by Peter Reynolds

Heinemann Educational
a division of Heinemann Publishers (Oxford) Ltd,
Halley Court, Jordan Hill, Oxford, OX2 8EJ

OXFORD LONDON EDINBURGH
MADRID ATHENS BOLOGNA PARIS
MELBOURNE SYDNEY AUCKLAND SINGAPORE TOKYO
IBADAN NAIROBI HARARE GABORONE
PORTSMOUTH NH (USA)

First published 1995

95 96 97 98 10 9 8 7 6 5 4 3 2 1

ISBN 0 435 50543 2

Designed and typeset by Ken Vail Graphic Design
Illustrated by Rupert Besley, Brian Hoskin, Tony Jarmain, Sue King, Mike Lacey, David Lock, Nigel Paige, Graeme Morris (Ken Vail Graphic Design)
Printed in Spain by Mateu Cromo, S.A. Pinto (Madrid)

Acknowledgements
The project and publishers gratefully acknowledge the contribution made by the late Hilary Shuard.
For permission to reproduce the following photographs and copyright material the authors and publishers would like to thank :
p. 42 Our Price; pp. 81, 82 ACE Photo Agency;
The Guardian and The Sun for the reproduction of newspaper extracts.
HMSO for permission to reproduce the National Curriculum level descriptions.

Cover picture
What are the chances that lightning will strike the same place twice? Units 3 and 8 in this book look at the language of probability and at certain and unlikely events.

About this book

This book is part of the Nuffield National Curriculum Mathematics series. It will help you learn mathematics and we hope you will enjoy using it.

How this book is organized

There are nine units of work in this book. They are numbered Unit 1 to Unit 9. Each unit provides information for you to read and questions and activities for you to do.

The units are presented in short sections. Each section has a letter and a title. For example, Section B of Unit 2 has the title:

B Three kinds of average

The questions and activities in Section B are numbered **B1**, **B2**, **B3** and so on to help you find them easily

The contents list on the next page shows you where each unit and section starts and tells you what mathematics they cover.

Symbols used in the Nuffield books

These symbols are shown in the margin of your book whenever you need worksheets, equipment or access to a computer:

H1:4

this means you need worksheet H1.4 from the Assessment and Resource Pack.

protractor
compass

you need equipment listed between the lines

spreadsheet

you need access to a computer and the software shown

Contents

UNIT 1 Collecting data

A Popularity polls

Mohammed, James and Tonia are collecting some information by asking people questions. Each time someone gives an answer they add a vertical tally mark to their recording sheet, with a horizontal bar for every fifth tally mark. Then they count the tally marks.

A1 What question do you think they asked?

A2 Why might they have wanted the information?

A3 How many people do you think they asked?

A4 They display the information in various ways.

Do you think some of these ways are better than others?
If so, explain why.

Information collected like this is called **data**.

A5 Conduct a popularity poll of your own.

If you have done this before, try to make this one more of a challenge so that you have to think more carefully what to do. For example, you could ask more people or ask more detailed questions.

When you have collected the data, try different ways of displaying it. Choose the best type of graph to present your data on graph paper.

You might think of using a pictogram. This uses a picture of a person to represent a number of people, like this:

each symbol stands for 10 people

B The throw of the dice

In this book the word dice is used to mean a single die or several dice.

Sheba and Richard do an experiment throwing two dice.

Each time they record the *total* number of dots shown on the two dice.

Here are their results:

6	11	9	5	5	12	6	12	8	3
8	8	5	9	10	4	7	7	8	4
7	7	10	9	7	5	8	6	7	12
7	4	8	5	8	5	10	9	7	9
7	9	6	7	5	2	9	4	8	7
6	5	6	9	6	3	9	9	10	6
7	5	2	4	11	7	4	3	6	9
4	3	8	5	8	12	7	7	3	6
9	6	6	10	7	10	6	7	6	7
7	2	6	5	11	6	9	6	7	9

They make a table:

Score	Tally marks	Frequency
2	𝍷𝍷𝍷	3
3	𝍸	5
4	𝍸 𝍷𝍷	7
5	𝍸 𝍸 𝍷	11
6	𝍸 𝍸 𝍸 𝍷𝍷	17
7	𝍸 𝍸 𝍸 𝍸	20
8	𝍸 𝍸	10
9	𝍸 𝍸 𝍷𝍷𝍷𝍷	14
10	𝍸 𝍷	6
11	𝍷𝍷𝍷	3
12	𝍷𝍷𝍷𝍷	4
Total		**100**

Each score is recorded by a tally mark.

They display the results in two ways:

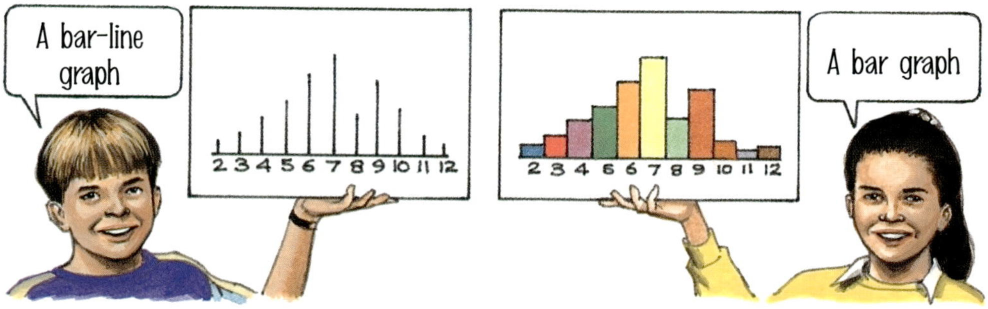

B1 Carry out the same experiment with two dice. Display the results in two ways. Are your results similar to those of Sheba and Richard?

Extension work

B2 Repeat the investigation, but use three, four or more dice.

Before you start, think what will be the largest and the smallest scores that you can get.

B3 To complete your experiment, repeat it with one dice.

What do you notice about the shapes of the graphs?

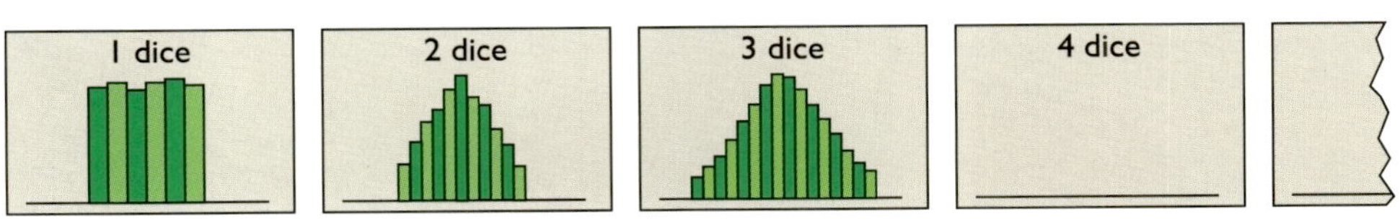

C Setting up shop

Imagine that you are setting up a shop.

C1 A market research company offers its services to you.

a Draw up a list of questions you would like answered before you go ahead. You could start with the ones on the previous page.
Which questions do you think the company could answer for you?

b Which of your questions would be easy to answer?
Which questions would be difficult or expensive to answer?

C2 Design a simple questionnaire for the market research company to use.

D Looking for trouble

D1 Line graphs are used to give a picture of what is happening.

The examples here show:

- a patient's temperature chart in hospital
- the sales made by a sales person over two years.

Write down some more examples where graphs are used to give a picture of what is happening, for example, in weather records.

In each case, say exactly what is being recorded.

D2 Here are the output figures for a cheese factory given in tonnes produced, for one week:

Week 1				
Mon	Tue	Wed	Thu	Fri
12	14	14	13	13

Plot these figures on a line graph. Choose the most suitable graph paper.

D3 Here are the figures for the second week:

Week 2

Mon	Tue	Wed	Thu	Fri
24	28	29	27	25

Plot a graph showing both weeks together, one after the other. Again choose the most suitable graph paper.

D4 Here are the figures for the third week:

Week 3

Mon	Tue	Wed	Thu	Fri
24	23	21	17	13

Now plot a graph to show all three weeks.

D5 Think of possible reasons for the different shape of the last graph. Are there any signs of possible trouble?

Extension question

D6 Find something you can measure every day at school, or at home. Record your measurements on a graph.

E Month by month

Rainfall statistics

Here are the monthly rainfall figures, in millimetres, for London:

Jan	Feb	Mar	Apr	May	Jun	Jul	Aug	Sep	Oct	Nov	Dec
54	40	37	37	46	45	57	59	49	57	64	48

Source: Guinness UK Data Book

You can show these figures on a bar graph:

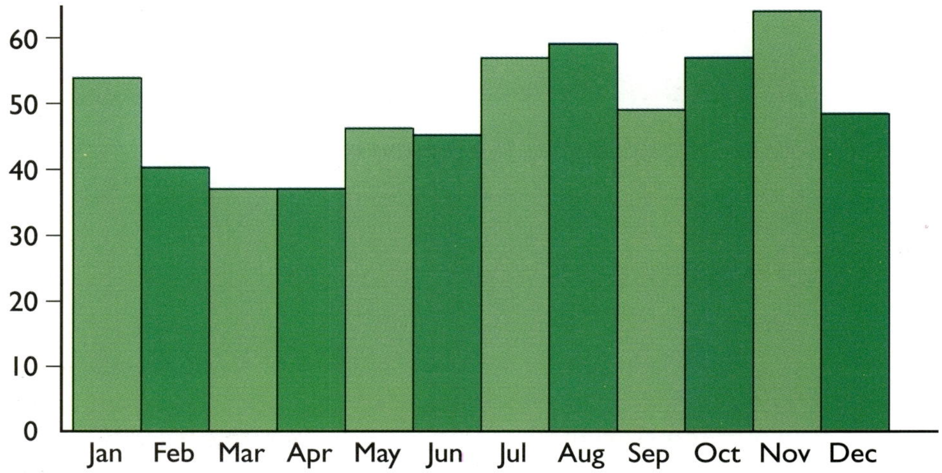

Here are the rainfall figures for two places in Africa:

Freetown

Jan	Feb	Mar	Apr	May	Jun	Jul	Aug	Sep	Oct	Nov	Dec
10	10	30	100	280	500	900	930	700	370	130	30

Timbuktu

Jan	Feb	Mar	Apr	May	Jun	Jul	Aug	Sep	Oct	Nov	Dec
0	0	10	0	20	28	85	50	21	20	0	0

Source: Philips Modern School Atlas

E1 Make bar graphs for the rainfall in Freetown and Timbuktu.

atlas

E2 When you have finished the bar graphs, look at a map of Africa. Explain why the figures are so different.

Months of birth

E3 Carry out a survey to find out the months of birth of people in your class or some other people.

Present your results as a bar graph.

Does your data support the idea that more people are born in winter?

E4 **Extension work:** Did you split the year up into two periods of six months? What happens if you split the year up into four periods of three months to coincide with the seasons? Make a new graph.

E5 Think of some other data that might usefully be collected month by month, such as the number of absences in your class or the number of school dinners taken. Think of reasons for collecting the data.

E6 Take one set of monthly statistics that you have already used. Present it as a bar-line graph instead of a bar graph. Which kind of graph do you think is better?

UNIT 2 What is the average?

A Why use averages?

You will hear lots of talk about **average**, but what does it mean?

Often it means some kind of middle value. So someone of average height is not tall and not short.

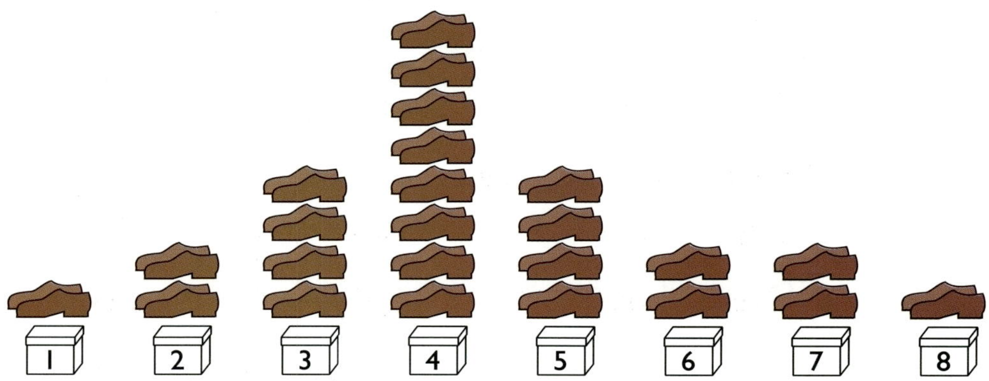

Sometimes it means the commonest value. For example, a shoe shop needs to know the commonest shoe size.

In this Unit we look at different meanings of the word average. Each kind of average is important in different circumstances.

A1 Write down three situations where you use the word average.

Did you think of average speed, average height, average age, average score, average marks, average attendance, a good average or average health?

We use the word average in many different ways. If it is your job to order stock for the school tuckshop, you need to know what the average pupil wants to buy. If you want to calculate how long a journey will take, you use the average speed. The size of the furniture in your classroom depends on the average size of pupils.

B Three kinds of average

When most people talk of average they think of what is more accurately called the **mean**.

Suppose three pupils have 75p, £1.10 and £1.15. You can work out the average money, or mean amount, that one pupil has by adding up the three amounts and dividing the total by three.

The mean amount of money is:

(75p + £1.10 + £1.15) ÷ 3 = £3.00 ÷ 3 = £1.00.

Notice that none of the three pupils actually has the average amount!

You could work out the mean height of the eleven children in the picture on the opposite page by adding up their heights to find a total height and dividing that by 11. But you can find a more sensible average by taking the height of the middle child, the sixth one along the line. We call this average the **median** or middle value.

It would not be sensible for the owner of a shoe shop to find the mean shoe size of customers: nobody has size 6.83 feet! She needs to know what are the most *popular* sizes and in particular the commonest size of her customers' feet. This commonest size is another kind of average, called the **mode**.

You will learn more about these different kinds of average in this Unit.

C The mean

C1 If the books were re-arranged with the same number in each pile, how many would there be in each pile?

One method of solving problems like this is:

Total number of books = 9 + 15 + 18 = 42

Number in each pile = 42 ÷ 3 = 14

This number is the mean.

The mean is what you would get if all the values were made equal.

Here is another question like question **C1**:

C2 Find the mean number of books in four piles of books if the piles contain 10 books, 7 books, 5 books and 6 books.

C3 Calculate the mean height of plants with heights 11 cm, 13 cm, 17 cm, 19 cm and 25 cm.

C4 This table shows a person's journey time for each day of the working week.

Mon	20 mins
Tue	22
Wed	24
Thur	23
Fri	21

What is the mean journey time for the week?

C5 Find the mean of each of the following sets of numbers:

a 10, 12, 16, 18, 24

b 11, 13, 17, 19, 25

c 20, 22, 24, 23, 21, 19, 18

d 3, 6, 12, 15

C6 **a** Write down a set of different numbers that have a mean of 15.

b Write down another set with the same mean.

c Investigate other sets of numbers with a mean of 15 and write down all you discover.

C7 On John's birthday the postman delivers ten envelopes and packets. He notices that the value of the stamps on each item is as follows:

24p, 18p, 24p, 58p, 18p, 36p, 41p, 85p, 18p, 18p

Mary receives eight envelopes and packets on her birthday. The stamps are for the following values:

24p, 18p, 18p, 74p, 66p, 18p, 28p, 18p

Who has envelopes and packets with stamps of the higher average value?

C8 Two evening newspapers are printed on six evenings each week.

The number of pages in each issue for one week is as follows:

	Mon	**Tue**	**Wed**	**Thu**	**Fri**	**Sat**
Gossip	48	52	56	52	60	44
Gasbag	48	64	52	48	48	40

Which newspaper has the bigger average number of pages for the week?

D The mode

The mode is usually the easiest average to find. It is the commonest value. For example, ten girls have shoe sizes

4, 3, 1, 4, 2, 4, 4, 6, 2 ,4

You can use a tally chart like those you used in Unit 1:

Size	Tally marks	Number
1	|	1
2	||	2
3	|	1
4	~~||||~~	5
5		0
6	|	1

It is obvious that the commonest shoe size is 4.

We say that the mode is 4.

D1 Find the mode for the following shoe sizes:

a 3, 3, 1, 6, 5, 3, 4, 2, 2, 3

b 5, 6, 4, 1, 3, 2, 3, 4, 2, 4, 4, 2, 4, 5, 3

D2 The ages of the first 20 people going into a youth club are:

12, 14, 13, 15, 13, 12, 13, 15, 16, 13, 13, 12, 13, 16, 14, 12, 14, 15, 13, 14

Find the mode.

D3 What is the mode in each of the following sets of numbers?

a 15, 17, 15, 15, 25, 15, 15, 15, 15, 15, 5

b 21, 21, 21, 23, 21, 21, 20, 21, 21, 21, 21, 19, 21

c 16, 16, 15, 16, 16, 16, 15, 16, 16, 16, 16

d 16, 15, 15, 15, 16, 15, 15, 15, 15, 15, 15

D4 Write down a set of numbers with a mode of 7.
Then write another set with the same mode.

D5 What is the mode of the shoe sizes for this group of children? Is it 6 or 20?

Size	Frequency
4	1
5	7
6	20
7	2
Total	30

(If you are unsure, make a list of the shoe sizes for all 30 children.)

D6 Is it possible to have a set of numbers in which the mode is exactly the same as the mean?

Is it possible for the mode to be greater than the mean?

Is it possible for it to be less?

5, 7, 8, 8, 9, 8

mode = 8

mean = 7.5

D7 What do you think is the correct answer to the teacher's question?

D8 Make a quick guess at the average of these numbers.

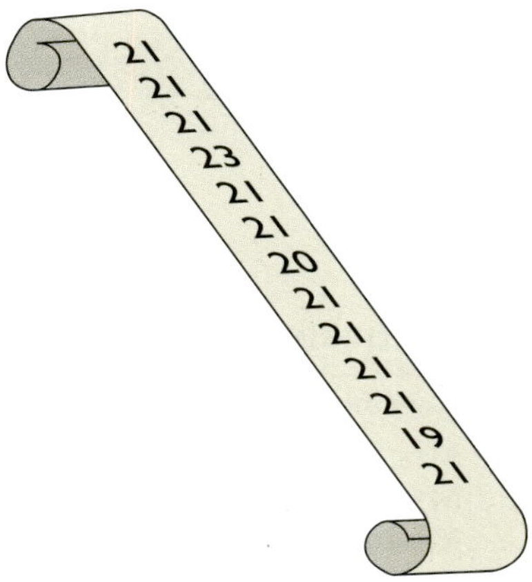

D9 Which team is older on average? How can you tell quickly?

	Name	*Age*		*Name*	*Age*
A team	A Brown	16	**B team**	J Joseph	16
	S Sekhri	16		D Kent	15
	...	15		...	15
	...	16		...	15
	...	16		...	16
	...	16		...	15
	...	15		...	15
	...	16		...	15
	...	16		...	15
	...	16		...	15
	...	16		...	15

E The median

The median is the middle value. You can only find it when you can put the data in order of size.

For example, when five pupils travel to school on Monday, the time that they take is 15 minutes, 17 minutes, 10 minutes, 12 minutes and 46 minutes.

If you put these times in order, shortest first, you get:

10, 12, 15, 17, 46

The middle value is 15 minutes.

This is called the median time. It gives a better idea of the average time then the mean time does. The mean time is 20 minutes because of the pupil who took very much longer than the average time.

The median value is the middle one when the values are listed in order of size.

E1 A small firm employs nine people.

The table shows their annual earnings to the nearest thousand pounds (£K).

Cook & Cook Ltd: Earnings (£K)

Mrs E Cook	30	Mrs J W Smith	13	Mr H Hatfield	10
Mr J Cook	30	Mrs V Hall	11	Mr W Jeavons	9
Mr K Jordan	14	Miss J Jarrett	10	Miss S Knowles	8

Make an estimate of the 'average' annual earnings. Do not calculate it yet. Write down your estimate.

E2 Find the median earnings for the people in question **E1**. Remember the figures are in thousands of pounds.

Mrs Hall comes in the middle.
Her earnings are £11K, that is, £11 000.
So the median is £11K or £11 000.

Everyone in the company has a pay rise

Cook & Cook Ltd: New Year's salaries (£K)

Mrs E Cook	31	Mrs J W Smith	14	Mr H Hatfield	11
Mr J Cook	31	Mrs V Hall	12	Mr W Jeavons	10
Mr K Jordan	15	Miss J Jarrett	11	Miss S Knowles	9

E3 Find the median earnings for this new list of salaries.

E4 Suppose that Cook & Cook Ltd take on two extra people, each earning £8K a year.

What difference would it make to the median of the New Year's salaries above?

E5 Try making other changes and calculate the effects.

F Various averages

Library opening hours

Westshire County Council
Magaton Branch
Opening hours

Mon	10.00–8.00	Thu	10.00–5.00
Tue	10.00–5.00	Fri	10.00–8.00
Wed	10.00–1.00	Sat	10.00–4.00

Westshire County Council
Miniton Branch
Opening hours

Tue	10.00–8.00	Fri	10.00–8.00
Wed	10.00–8.00	Sat	10.00–4.00
Thu	10.00–8.00	Closed Sun & Mon	

F1 Which branch has the longer opening hours?

F2 Work out the average number of hours per day for each branch.
Do you think that this is a useful figure? Why?

Days in the month

Thirty days has September,
April, June and November.
All the rest have thirty one,
excepting February alone,
which has but twenty eight days clear,
and twenty nine in each leap year.

F3 Calculate for a leap year:

a the average (mean) number of days in a month

b the mode

c the median.

2.4 children

F4 Does it make sense to speak of an average of 2.4 children? What could it mean?

The average family has 2.4 children

Admission prices

E5 *Is* the average price increase 30p?

E6 Suppose that 100 people buy tickets: 90 at full price, 10 as students or pensioners.

- **a** How much extra money will the hall take as a result of the price increase?
- **b** How much is this per person?

Here is a skating competition:

E7 Check that the mean is indeed 6.

E8 What would be the mean if the scores were 8, 4, 6, 8, 4?

E9 Make up another set of five scores so that the mean is still 6.

UNIT 3 *Is it likely?*

A A simple game

counter or coin

HI:1 HI:2

You need:

- a board like the one opposite
- a marker such as a small counter or coin
- a pile of cards labelled LEFT, RIGHT and FORWARD.

First get the cards. Your teacher may have some or you can make them.

You should have 24 cards, all the same size and colour: eight marked LEFT, eight RIGHT and eight FORWARD.

To play:

- place the marker on START
- shuffle the cards in a pile face downwards
- take the top card and move the counter one square according to the instructions on the card
- then put the card at the bottom of the pile.

Play the game several times. Note what happens.

Then change the game by altering the number of cards or the size of the board or …

Here are some challenges:

- arrange things so that you are bound to lose or bound to win
- arrange things so that you are equally likely to win or lose
- arrange things so that you nearly always lose.

The game board

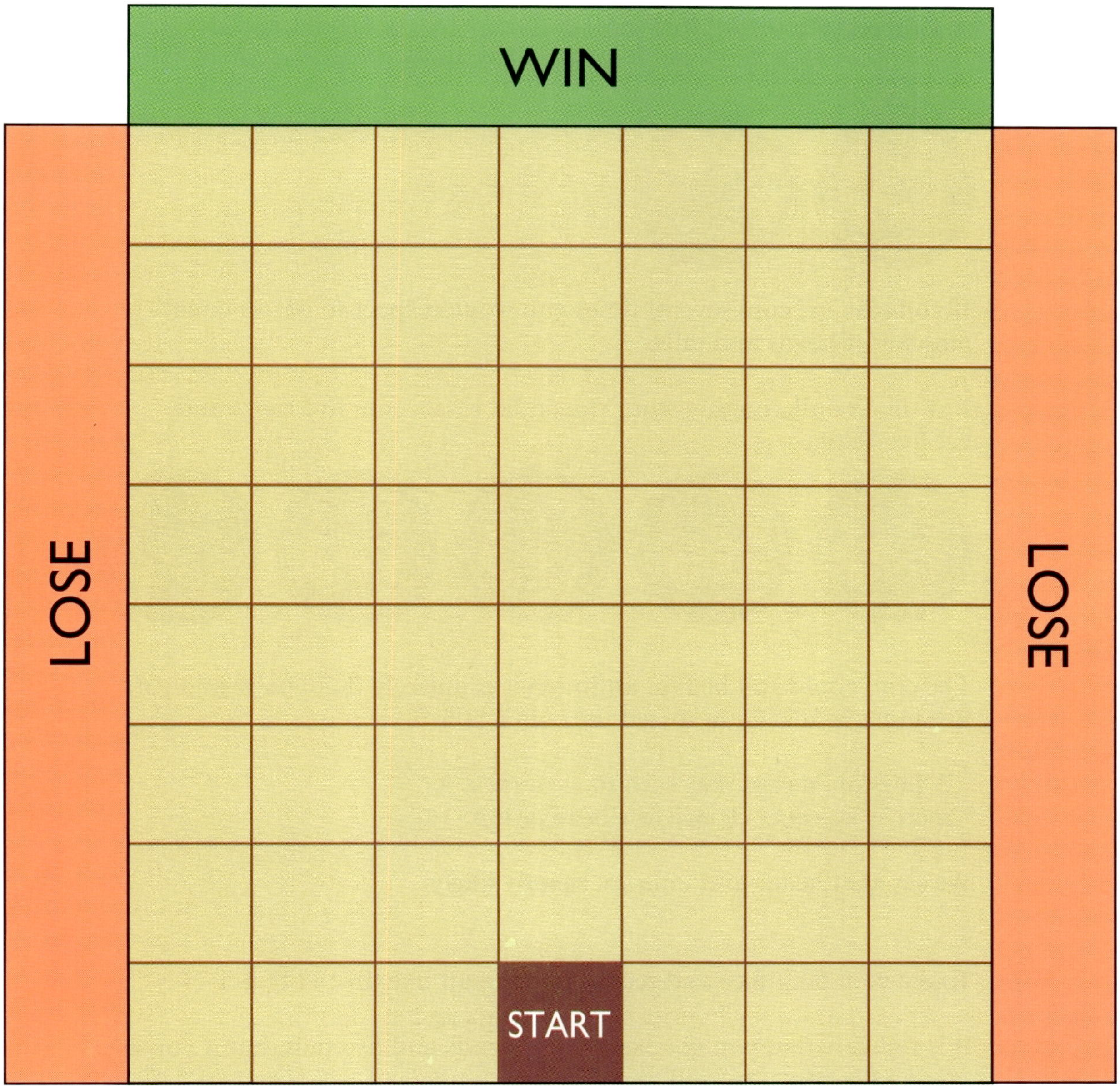

B Is it fair?

A fair coin

A coin has two sides: a head and a tail.

If you toss the coin several times you would expect to get an equal number of heads and tails.

But this is only roughly true. You could toss a coin five times and get five heads.

The coin could still be fair, although it is unlikely that you would get five more heads if you tossed the coin again.

A fair coin means that each time you toss it there is an equal chance of a head or tail.

We say that heads and tails are **equally likely**.

coin

B1 Toss a coin ten times and record your result like this: H H T T H …

It is unlikely that you got exactly five heads and five tails, but if you keep tossing the coin, you will find that the numbers of heads and tails *are* roughly the same.

A fair dice

A dice has six faces with the numbers 1, 2, 3, 4, 5 and 6 on them.

A fair dice means that every one of the numbers is equally likely to occur when you roll it. Many young children think that it is harder to get a six than any other number, because a lot of board games need a six to start and often it needs several turns before a six appears.

dice

B2 **a** Take a dice and roll it 60 times.
Record your results on a tally sheet like this:

Number	Tally marks	Total
1		
2		
3		
4		
5		
6		

You are unlikely to get *exactly* ten of each number, but usually you will get about ten of each number.

b Repeat the experiment. Do you get the same result or a similar result? Are you convinced that your dice is fair?

Beads in a bag

Suppose you put some beads which are identical except for colour into a bag so that you cannot see the beads. Then take one bead out. The colour of that bead depends on the number and colour of the beads you put into the bag.

If five red and five blue beads are put into a bag and one is drawn out, it is equally likely that the bead will be red or blue. You can test this by an experiment.

bag
10 beads

B3 Put ten beads in a bag, five of one colour and five of another colour.

Take out a bead and record its colour.

Put the bead back in the bag and shake the bag.

Repeat the process until you have recorded the colour of ten beads.

You know the bag is fair, but did you get roughly five of each colour?

C The future

Here are some possible events:

A It will rain tomorrow

B I will be younger tomorrow than I am today

C I will come to school tomorrow

D The Queen will appear on TV tomorrow

C1 **a** Which do you think is more likely, A or C?

b Which is more likely, C or B?

c Compare all possible pairs. State which is more likely in each case. (Make sure that you include every possible pair – you should have six.)

Write your answers like this:

I think A is more likely than B
B is more likely than
A is more likely

C2 Write all four events in order starting with the least likely.

B least likely

☐

☐

☐ most likely

C3 Draw a **probability line** and mark events where you think they should come on the scale.

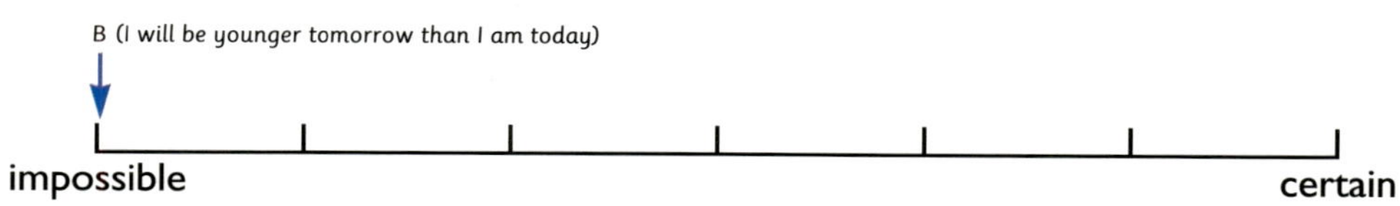

C4 Compare these in pairs: A and B, A and C, A and D, B and C, B and D, C and D. State which you think is more likely for each pair.

A I will become a doctor

B I will get married

C I will become a parent

D I will become famous

C5 Write A, B, C and D in order starting with the least likely.

C6 Make a probability line like this and mark A, B, C and D on it:

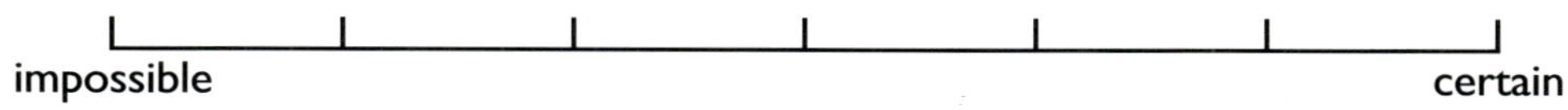

C7 **a** Make up some possible events. Work in groups if possible.

A

B

C

D

E

F

b Compare the events two at a time.

c Write them in order of probability.

d Mark them on a probability line.

D The dice line

Here are some possible results when you roll a dice:

- A roll a 6
- B roll a 5
- C roll an odd number
- D roll a 7
- E roll a 1
- F roll an even number
- G roll a number bigger than 4

D1 **a** Which of these events is least likely?

b Which is most likely?

c Which, if any, are equally likely?

D2 Write the seven events A, B, C, D, E, F and G in order starting with the least likely.
(If two are equally likely, show this in a suitable way.)

D3 Draw a probability line like the one below. The event D (roll a 7) has been marked on it.

Mark the other six events on your line.

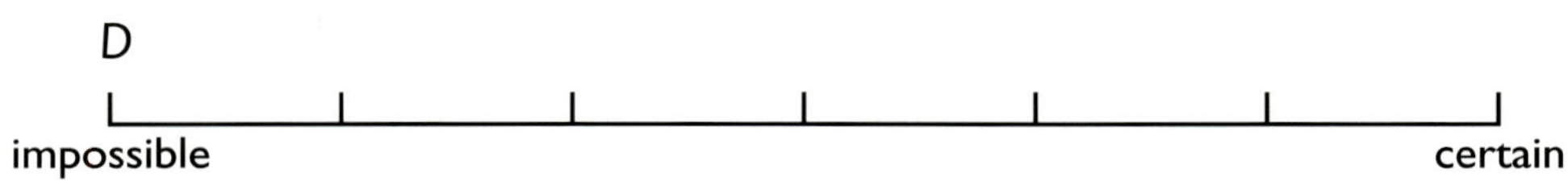

D4 Think of some more possible events to add to your probability line.

- H
- I
- J

dice

D5 Take a real dice and test how your ideas work out in practice.

An unusual dice

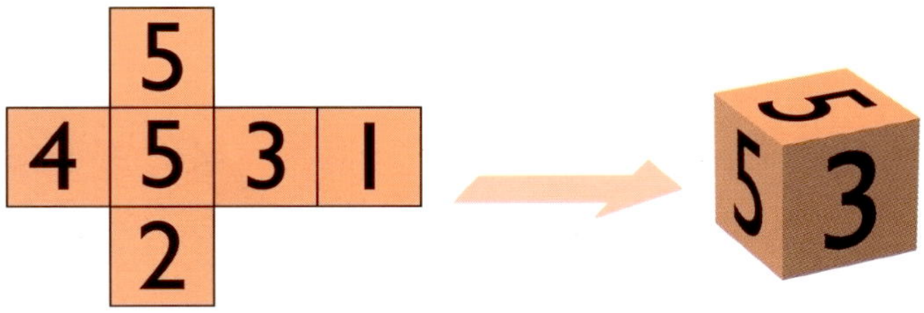

D6 Look at these possibilities for this dice:

- A roll a 6
- B roll a 5
- C roll an odd number
- D roll a 7
- E roll a 1
- F roll an even number
- G roll a number bigger than 4

Make a probability line and mark different possibilities. (You might like to make a dice like this using Plasticine or a wooden cube and test it out.)

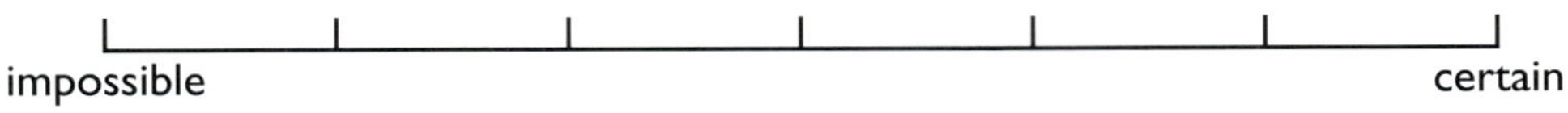

D7 Create your own unusual dice. Make a probability line showing various possible events.

E Drawing pins

E1 If you drop a drawing pin, it will land in one of two possible ways:

point up *point down*

Which do you think is more likely?

drawing pins

E2 Carry out an experiment to answer question **E1**.
You could drop ten drawing pins each time and record the number of pins that land point up.

E3 Repeat the experiment to see if you get the same answer. If not, why do you think you got a different answer?

E4 From your experiment, how likely is it that a drawing pin will land point up? Where would you mark this on a probability line?

E5 Some children do an experiment using drawing pins of various colours. the results are:

Colour	Up	Down
black	10	3
blue	8	5
green	8	5
mauve	6	6
orange	5	7
red	8	4
white	8	5
yellow	8	4

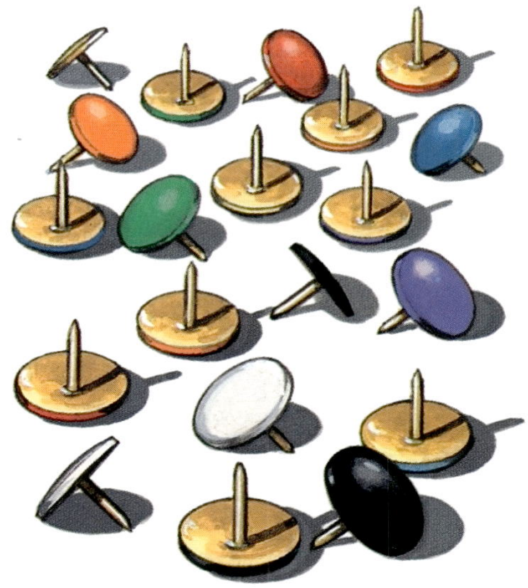

Do you think that there might be a difference in the shapes of coloured drawing pins?

E6 Do you think that their drawing pins are similar to yours?

E7 The children repeat their experiment:

Colour	Up	Down
black	6	6
blue	8	5
green	7	6
mauve	8	5
orange	6	6
red	6	6
white	6	7
yellow	6	6

Do these results confirm what you thought before, or do they make you change your mind?
Explain.

UNIT 4 Presenting data

A Out of the hat

Here are some experiments about drawing numbers out of a hat. The numbers are put back in the hat before the next number is drawn.

Experiment 1: small numbers

In the hat are the numbers 1, 2, 3, 4, 5, 6, 7, 8 and 9.

Pat and Chris make 100 draws. Here are their results:

3	5	6	9	3	6	8	7	9	4	3	2	9	8	4	8	3	1	5	5
9	8	1	5	4	3	3	4	6	6	1	7	9	1	5	8	3	7	6	2
8	7	7	3	7	2	1	6	8	1	5	7	1	4	2	3	3	3	3	9
2	6	9	7	5	3	5	4	7	7	7	8	6	2	2	1	9	1	9	4
2	9	5	7	8	8	4	7	5	1	4	1	7	5	1	4	8	1	2	5

They make a table and a bar graph

Number	Tally marks	Frequency
1	𝍸 𝍸 |||	13
2	𝍸 ||||	9
3	𝍸 𝍸 |||	13
4	𝍸 𝍸	10
5	𝍸 𝍸 ||	12
6	𝍸 |||	8
7	𝍸 𝍸 ||||	14
8	𝍸 𝍸		11
9	𝍸 𝍸	10
Total		100

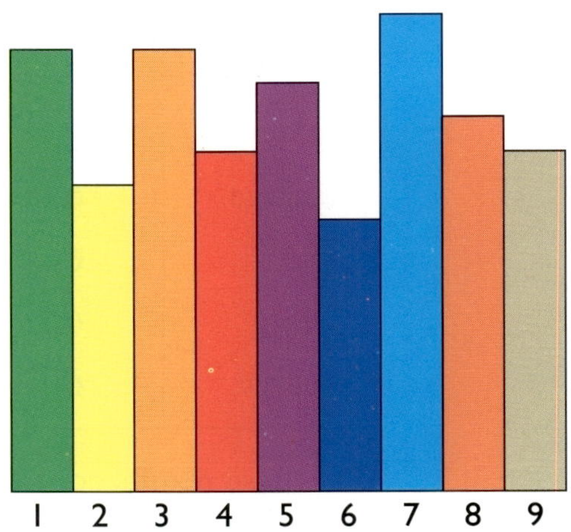

A1 Repeat this experiment yourself before going on to Experiment 2. Compare your results with those above.

Experiment 2: numbers 1 to 60

This time the hat contains 60 slips of paper numbered 1–60. Pat and Chris make 100 draws. Here are their results:

43	30	36	14	10	7	16	21	29	45	7	8	25	4	46	5	41	4	60	34
40	50	44	32	39	7	60	49	20	51	4	50	34	9	15	2	5	40	24	19
27	10	32	8	2	59	27	34	46	60	31	40	38	3	26	15	6	34	60	12
15	60	50	35	19	55	48	12	16	26	40	18	20	59	47	14	33	3	33	52
13	44	41	34	29	59	17	52	60	59	40	14	53	17	44	25	37	51	57	35

Before making a bar graph, they **group** the data:

Number	Tally marks	Frequency
1–10	𝍸 𝍸 𝍸 𝍷𝍷𝍷	18
11–20	𝍸 𝍸 𝍸 𝍷𝍷𝍷	18
21–30	𝍸 𝍸 𝍷	11
31–40	𝍸 𝍸 𝍸 𝍸 𝍷	21
41–50	𝍸 𝍸 𝍸	15
51–60	𝍸 𝍸 𝍸 𝍷𝍷	17

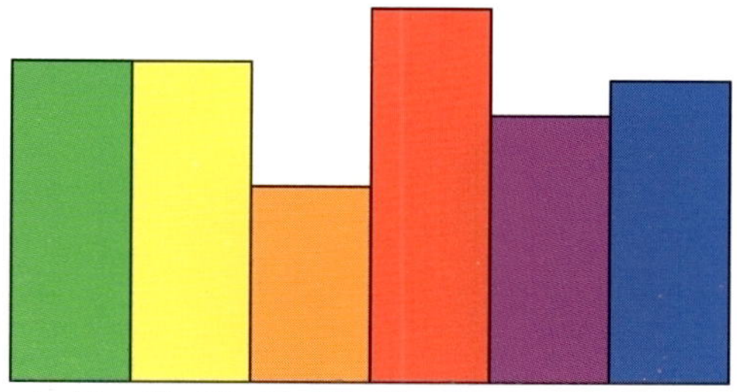

A2 What will happen if you make a bar graph without grouping the data? If you are not sure, try it.

A3 Find another way of grouping this data and make a new bar graph.

A4 Find a third way of grouping this data and make a third bar graph.

Experiment 3: other sets of random numbers

A5 Do the same with other sets of numbers. Either use the data below or do your own experiments to produce numbers. For example, you might use the last digit of telephone numbers in a telephone directory. You might also use a computer or calculator to generate the data.

In each case, group the data in the way you think best. Try different ways of grouping and see if it makes much difference to the bar graph.

Data 1: numbers 1 to 36

19	18	10	27	26	6	9	22	10	35	7	9	27	35	19	10	20	6	22	13
32	1	9	23	1	11	36	23	25	33	17	12	25	35	18	19	25	3	9	33
29	28	11	8	27	17	21	23	15	32	30	10	18	24	36	9	25	21	35	21
33	34	5	28	16	13	35	13	16	30	10	36	3	34	27	35	5	25	1	23
29	1	10	21	25	23	30	6	30	36	12	20	1	20	30	13	13	10	31	33

Data 2: numbers 0 to 99

11	91	6	33	83	19	74	10	64	37	49	5	11	81	34	58	29	40	97	71
72	73	43	51	85	69	71	28	44	73	73	34	47	32	24	1	61	24	28	53
13	61	55	48	33	18	96	61	40	44	32	17	31	41	1	91	60	39	48	74
91	42	70	25	50	83	16	12	89	43	92	90	27	78	10	89	37	70	82	77
96	54	27	57	17	10	75	64	53	45	3	11	46	63	96	81	63	69	50	42

B TV and radio audiences

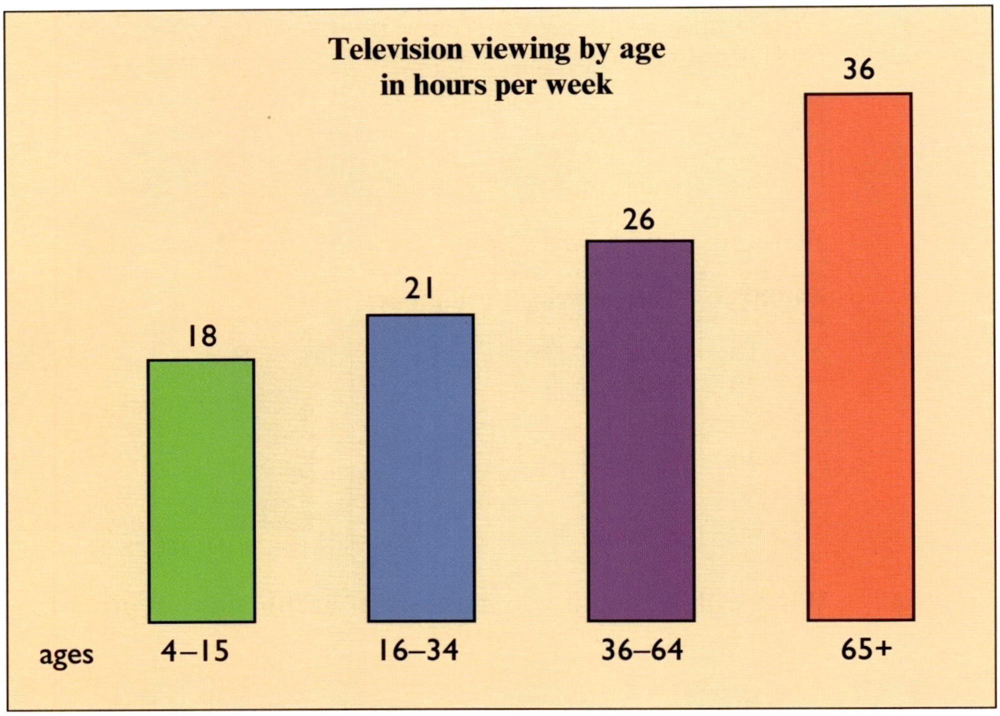

Source: Guinness UK Data Book

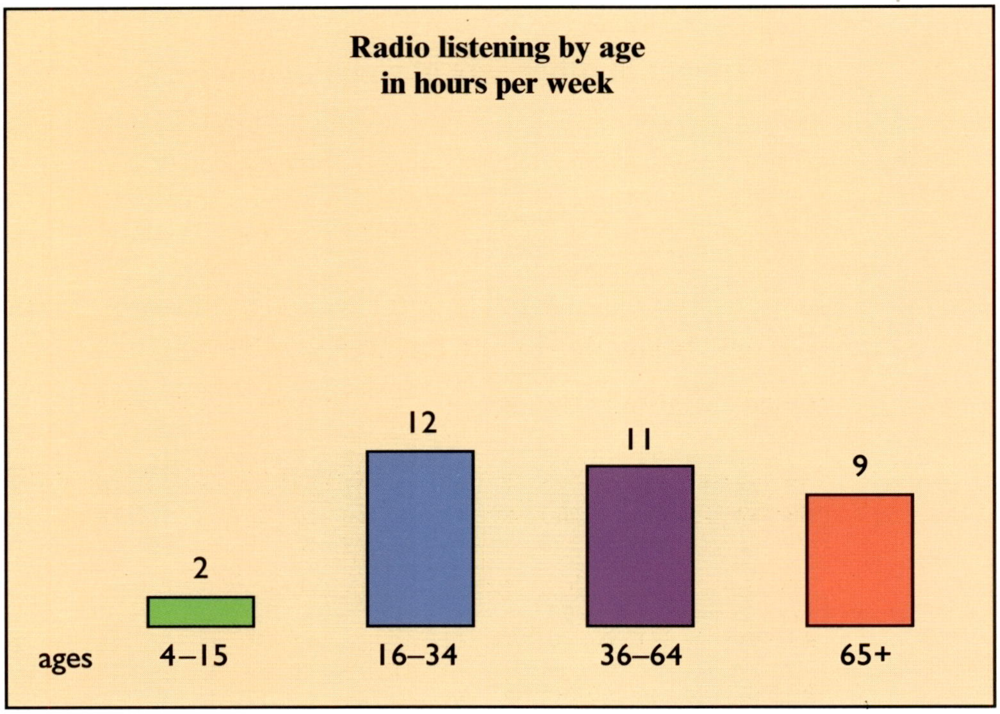

Source: Guinness UK Data Book

B1 Study the two sets of findings shown opposite.

Write a few sentences about them. Mention anything you find surprising and anything you would have expected.

B2 **a** How do you think these figures were obtained?

b Do you think they are reliable? Explain your answer.

B3 How would you set about checking whether the figures apply to the people you know or meet?

You may wish to do a survey, but decide beforehand:

- what you need to find out
- what you need to ask
- how you will show your results.

C Beads in a bottle

In a competition at a school fete, people have to guess how many beads there are in a bottle. Richard and Emily investigate the answers people give.

Here are the answers given by 100 people:

65	67	69	74	63	66	64	59	63	72	69	63	71	70	60	56	74	63	64	64
75	71	62	69	60	64	67	71	70	61	62	61	68	69	73	66	68	68	60	67
69	65	65	60	73	60	64	77	69	66	65	74	66	56	54	65	62	62	67	74
60	67	60	61	67	66	62	72	69	58	70	69	65	73	64	71	68	67	70	62
62	66	73	71	58	72	73	71	65	68	63	64	64	67	64	63	70	54	64	62

At first, Richard and Emily grouped the data and made a bar graph like this:

Number	Tally marks	Frequency
50–59	𝍸 ||	7
60–69	𝍸 𝍸 𝍸 𝍸 𝍸 𝍸 𝍸 𝍸 𝍸 𝍸 𝍸 𝍸 𝍸 |||	68
70–79	𝍸 𝍸 𝍸 𝍸 𝍸	25
80–89		0

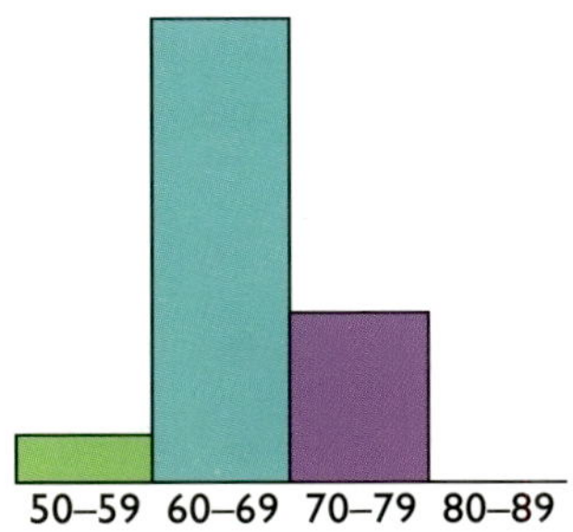

But then they thought it would be better to have different groupings.

C1 Copy and complete this table.

Number	Tally marks	Frequency
50–54		
55–59		
60–64		
65–69		
70–74		
75–79		

Make a bar graph.
Do you think it is better than the first graph?

Here are some more estimates:

Data 1

48	49	52	49	49	52	51	49	50	49	49	50	50	51	52	52	49	51	50	50
51	51	51	49	51	50	50	49	50	51	49	49	48	49	51	50	49	51	50	49
51	51	51	53	50	51	50	47	50	53	49	50	52	49	48	49	51	50	50	48
49	51	51	50	51	52	52	48	51	48	51	49	49	50	50	52	49	50	49	49
53	50	52	48	49	49	51	49	52	51	50	49	49	52	52	49	50	48	49	51

Data 2

48	50	53	49	49	50	49	49	49	52	49	52	51	51	48	54	54	54	47	54
51	51	51	48	46	54	52	55	53	50	50	53	50	56	50	49	51	48	48	52
47	49	50	51	47	54	49	48	52	47	51	49	48	50	52	48	48	53	56	51
54	48	53	50	52	49	50	49	53	54	55	51	54	48	51	48	53	49	56	50
53	54	54	51	50	51	52	47	50	54	53	48	52	47	56	51	49	51	45	45

Data 3

54	54	60	50	51	56	54	46	54	54	53	60	56	51	49	52	52	50	49	49
50	55	57	57	48	55	51	50	46	55	55	52	50	48	58	50	56	58	51	52
57	52	56	56	51	60	59	52	56	59	51	55	58	51	61	54	56	54	47	59
56	56	56	52	55	51	52	55	50	57	51	54	55	55	51	58	50	56	51	54
55	52	56	51	54	47	52	56	52	59	49	55	55	57	48	52	51	55	57	57

C2 Take one or more of these sets of data and make a bar graph. Group the data in the way you think best.

Try more than one way of grouping and see which gives the best graph.

C3 Think of some more situations that would give a bar graph of the same humped shape as the estimates of beads in a bottle.

D Line graphs

D1 This table shows the average daily maximum temperatures for each month of the year in London in degrees Celsius (°C).

Make a line graph to show this data.

Jan	Feb	Mar	Apr	May	Jun	Jul	Aug	Sep	Oct	Nov	Dec
6	7	10	13	17	20	22	21	19	14	10	7

Source: Guinness UK Data Book

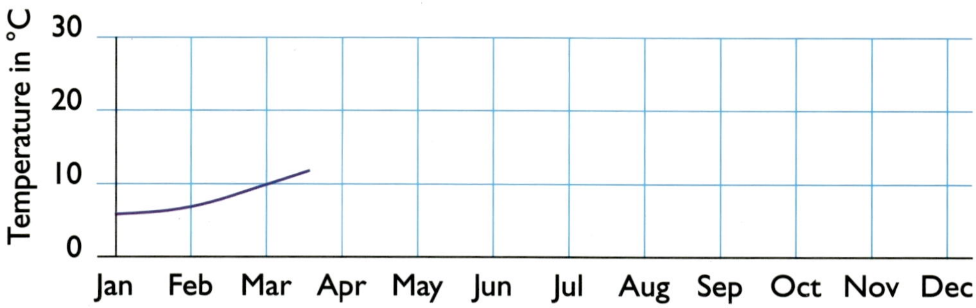

D2 Here is the monthly temperature data for Alice Springs in the centre of Australia:

Jan	Feb	Mar	Apr	May	Jun	Jul	Aug	Sep	Oct	Nov	Dec
36	35	32	26	21	19	19	22	25	31	32	36

Source: Philips Modern School Atlas

a Make a line graph for this data.

b Write a few sentences comparing the two graphs.

D3 Here is data on times of sunset in England at or near the beginning of each month. The times are given to the nearest quarter of an hour.

Month	Sunset	Month	Sunset
January	1600	July	2115
February	1700	August	2045
March	1745	September	1945
April	1930	October	1830
May	2030	November	1630
June	2115	December	1600

D4 Make a line graph to show the data.

D5 Extend your line graph to show what happens over two or more years.

D6 Make another graph to show what would happen if the clocks were not altered for British Summer Time.

D7 The takings in a large supermarket in thousands of pounds (£K) for a two-week period were:

Week 1		Week 2	
Monday	8	Monday	7
Tuesday	10	Tuesday	9
Wednesday	11	Wednesday	11
Thursday	13	Thursday	14
Friday	17	Friday	18
Saturday	15	Saturday	15

Make a bar graph like the one started below to represent the takings.

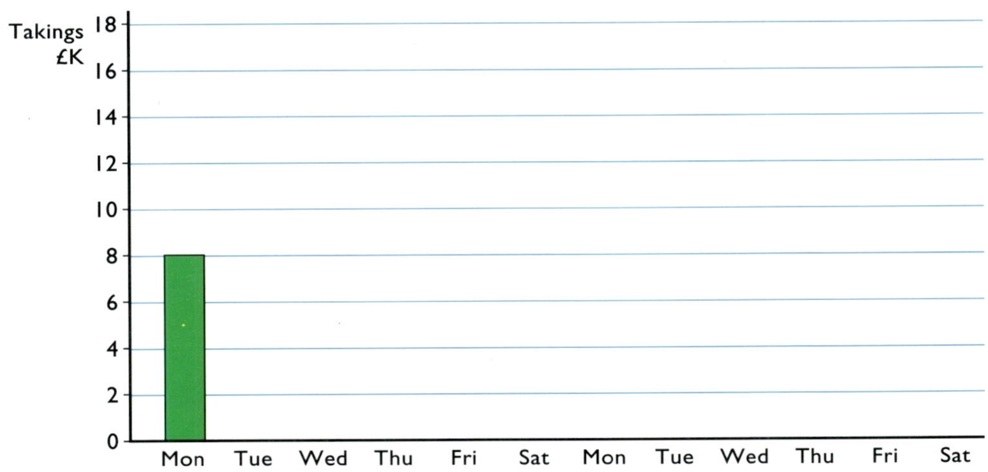

E Job advertisements

In the local newspaper, there are three and a half pages of advertisements headed *Recruitment*. Rani, Ann and Michael are studying them.

They find many difficulties in interpreting the information.

In the end they produce a report.

Job Advertisement in Banshire Gazette
Report by Rani, Ann and Michael
There were 85 ads. A lot of them were for sales persons.
Many of them did not give a salary or said it was negotiable. We grouped the salaries that were given like this:

Under £10K	9
£10–15K	12
£15–20K	7
Over £20K	5
Total	33

These are shown on a graph on the next page.

E1 Make your own survey of job advertisements and write a report. Include one or more graphs.

UNIT 5 Using databases

A What is a database?

spreadsheet
database

A database is way of storing information (data). You don't need a computer but a computer makes using databases much easier.

The simplest database is a plain card, like a postcard. It should have columns drawn on it for writing the data in.

You may wish to keep a note of all your records or tapes.
You would have to decide for each record what data to write down.
You might decide that you want four pieces of data for each one:

Artist	Title	Catalogue number	Price
Bloggs, Joe	I'm going pink	ABC 3476	£5.00

Each disc or tape would have its own card.

You could keep all your cards in a box:

You might then decide to sort the cards alphabetically by artist. The first card could be:

Artist	Title	Catalogue number	Price
Apple, Mac	Two true	XYZ 9876	£6.75

Or you might sort them by title so that the first card could be:

Artist	Title	Catalogue number	Price
Popcorn, Jo	Away I go	FGH 5674	£4.50

If you have more than ten cards to sort, you will find it takes a little time. Of course, if the data are put on a computer, sorting is very fast.

cards

A1 Make a few cards for your own collection of records or tapes or, if you prefer, cards on a different topic such as:

Football team	Player	Age	Number of games played

or:

TV programme title	What it's about	Channel	Time of showing

or one of your own.

Then sort your cards alphabetically using the first column.

You can also sort by the size of a number. For example, you could sort your cards of pop records or tapes by price, starting with the cheapest:

Artist	Title	Catalogue number	Price
Mole, Pat	Boring	QWE 0987	£0.50

In the next section you will look at a very large set of data on volcanoes.

B Volcanoes

Name	Location	Continent	Major eruptions	Last
Awu	Indonesia	Asia	1711, 1856, 1892	1968
Bezymianny	Russia	Asia	1955–6	1984
Cosequina	Nicaragua	S America	1835	1835
El Chichon	Mexico	S America	1982	1982
Erebus	Antarctica	Antarctica	1947, 1972	1986
Etna	Italy	Europe	122, 1169, 1329, 1536, 1669, 1928, 1964, 1971	1986
Fuiji	Japan	Asia	1707	1707
Galunggung	Java	Asia	1822, 1918	1982
Hekla	Iceland	Europe	1693, 1845, 1947–8, 1970	1981
Helgafell	Iceland	Europe	1973	1973
Jurullo	Mexico	S America	1759–74	1774
Katmai	Alaska	N America	1912, 1920 1921	1931
Kilauea	Hawaii	N America	1923–4, 1952, 1955, 1960, 1967–74, 1983–7	1991
Klyuchevskoy	Russia	Asia	1700–1966, 1984	1985
Krakatoa	Sumatra	Asia	1680, 1883, 1927, 1952–3, 1969	1980
La Soufrere	St Vincent	S America	1718, 1812, 1902, 1971–2	1979
Laki	Iceland	Europe	1783	1784
Lamington	Papua N Guinea	Asia	1951	1956
Lassen Peak	USA	N America	1914–5	1921
Mauna Loa	Hawaii	N America	1859, 1880, 1887, 1919, 1950	1984
Mayon	Philippines	Asia	1616, 1766, 1814, 1897, 1989	1978
Nyamuragira	Zaire	Africa	1921–38, 1971, 1980	1984
Paricutin	Mexico	S America	1943–52	1952
Pelee, Mont	Martinique	S America	1902, 1929–32	1932
Pinatubo, Mt	Philippines	Asia	1391, 1991	1991
Popocatepetl	Mexico	S America	1920	1943
Rainier, Mt	USA	N America	1820	1882
Ruapehu	New Zealand	Australasia	1945, 1953, 1969, 1975	1986
Santorini	Greece	Europe	1570–3, 1707–11, 1866–70	1950
St Helens, Mt	USA	N America	1800, 1831, 1835, 1842–3, 1857, 1980	1987
Stromboli	Italy	Europe	1768, 1882, 1889, 1907, 1930, 1941, 1950, 1952	1986
Surtsey	Iceland	Europe	1963–7	1967
Taal	Philippines	Asia	1911, 1965, 1969	1977
Tambora	Indonesia	Asia	1815	1880
Tarawera	New Zealand	Australasia	1886	1973
Unzen	Japan	Asia	1360, 1791	1991
Vesuvius	Italy	Europe	79, 472, 1036, 1631, 1779, 1906	1944
Vulcano	Italy	Europe	1444, 1730–40, 1786, 1873, 1888–90	1890

Source: Chambers Quick Facts

The table opposite gives information about major volcanoes in the world.

Karen and Ashmed have put this data into a computer. They instruct the computer to select the data in two different ways. They get these printouts:

Printout 1

Etna	Italy	Europe	122, 1169, 1329, 1536, 1669, 1928, 1964, 1971	1986
Hekla	Iceland	Europe	1693, 1845, 1947-8, 1970	1981
Helgafell	Iceland	Europe	1973	1973
Laki	Iceland	Europe	1783	1784
Santorini	Greece	Europe	1570-3, 1707-11, 1866-70	1950
Stromboli	Italy	Europe	1768, 1882, 1889, 1907, 1930, 1941, 1950, 1952	1986
Surtsey	Iceland	Europe	1963-7	1967
Vesuvius	Italy	Europe	79, 472, 1036, 1631, 1779, 1906	1944
Vulcano	Italy	Europe	1444, 1730-40, 1786, 1873, 1888-90	1890

Printout 2

Kilauea	Hawaii	N America	1923-4, 1952, 1955, 1960, 1967-74, 1983-7	1991
Pinatubo, Mt	Philippines	Asia	1391, 1991	1991
Unzen	Japan	Asia	1360, 1791	1991
St Helens, Mt	USA	N America	1800, 1831, 1835, 1842-3, 1857, 1980	1987
Erebus	Antarctica	Antarctica	1947, 1972	1986
Etna	Italy	Europe	122, 1169, 1329, 1536, 1669, 1928, 1964, 1971	1986
Ruapehu	New Zealand	Australasia	1945, 1953, 1969, 1975	1986
Stromboli	Italy	Europe	1768, 1882, 1889, 1907, 1930, 1941, 1950, 1952	1986
Klyuchevskoy	Russia	Asia	1700-1966, 1984	1985
Bezymianny	Russia	Asia	1955-6	1984
Mauna Loa	Hawaii	N America	1859, 1880, 1887, 1919, 1950	1984
Nyamuragira	Zaire	Africa	1921-38, 1971, 1980	1984
El Chichon	Mexico	S America	1982	1982
Galunggung	Java	Asia	1822, 1918	1982
Hekla	Iceland	Europe	1693, 1845, 1947-8, 1970	1981
Krakatoa	Sumatra	Asia	1680, 1883, 1927, 1952-3, 1969	1980
La Soufrere	St Vincent	S America	1718, 1812, 1902, 1971-2	1979
Mayon	Philippines	Asia	1616, 1766, 1814, 1897, 1989	1978
Taal	Philippines	Asia	1911, 1965, 1969	1977
Helgafell	Iceland	Europe	1973	1973
Tarawera	New Zealand	Australasia	1886	1973
Awu	Indonesia	Asia	1711, 1856, 1892	1968
Surtsey	Iceland	Europe	1963-7	1967
Lamington	Papua N Guinea	Asia	1951	1956
Paricutin	Mexico	S America	1943-52	1952
Santorini	Greece	Europe	1570-3, 1707-11, 1866-70	1950

B1 Look carefully at the printouts. Decide what information Karen and Ahmed instruct the computer to select for each.

B2 What other, similar printouts could you get from the same data?

C The class database

Miss Reed, who teaches class 7, keeps records on her computer of her pupils' attendance and the National Curriculum levels they have reached in each subject.

Here is the database for Class 7.

Class 7

surname	first name	gender	attendance	Eng	math	sci	tech	hist	geog	French	art	music	PE
Bentall	Felicity	f	45	4	4	5	5	3	4	4	4	4	4
Bordon	Alan	m	55	4	4	4	3	4	4	4	3	4	4
Byfleet	Shuman	m	47	4	4	4	4	5	4	5	3	2	4
Courtney	Cecil	m	50	6	6	6	4	5	4	4	3	4	4
English	Norma	f	47	7	6	6	5	5	5	5	3	4	4
German	Angela	f	50	7	7	6	7	6	4	4	3	4	4
Harriet	George	m	57	5	5	4	4	4	4	3	4	4	4
Hassan	Eliza	f	48	5	5	5	6	5	5	4	3	3	4
Holiday	Stephanie	f	50	4	4	3	3	4	4	5	4	3	5
Kassel	Honey	f	59	7	7	7	7	6	5	4	3	5	4
Knowles	Jennifer	f	27	3	3	3	3	4	6	4	4	2	3
Lane	Mary	f	54	5	5	5	5	5	4	3	3	5	4
McIntyre	Jack	m	52	4	4	4	4	5	4	4	3	3	5
McIntyre	Jill	f	54	5	5	4	4	5	5	5	5	2	4
Minor	Maurice	m	25	3	2	2	3	4	3	2	3	4	4
Moon	James	m	56	6	6	6	5	6	4	6	3	3	6
Orion	Frances	f	58	6	7	6	6	7	6	5	4	4	4
Pendang	Phui	f	55	5	6	5	5	6	4	5	5	2	4
Smith	Jennifer	f	52	3	3	3	4	4	4	3	3	3	4
York	Evans	m	49	6	6	6	6	6	5	5	3	4	4

Class 7

surname	first name	gender	attendance	Eng	math	sci	tech	hist	geog	French	art	music	PE
Bentall	Felicity	f	45	4	4	5	5	3	4	4	4	4	4
English	Norma	f	47	7	6	6	5	5	5	5	3	4	4
German	Angela	f	50	7	7	6	7	6	4	4	3	4	4
Hassan	Eliza	f	48	5	5	5	6	5	5	4	3	3	4
Holiday	Stephanie	f	50	4	4	3	3	4	4	5	4	3	5
Kassel	Honey	f	59	7	7	7	7	6	5	4	3	5	4
Knowles	Jennifer	f	27	3	3	3	3	4	6	4	4	2	3
Lane	Mary	f	54	5	5	5	5	5	4	3	3	5	4
Mcintyre	Jill	f	54	5	5	4	4	5	5	5	5	2	4
Orion	Frances	f	58	6	7	6	6	7	6	5	4	4	4
Pendang	Phui	f	55	5	6	5	5	6	4	5	5	2	4
Smith	Jennifer	f	52	3	3	3	4	4	4	3	3	3	4
Bordon	Alan	m	55	4	4	4	3	4	4	4	3	4	4
Byfleet	Shuman	m	47	4	4	4	4	5	4	5	3	2	4
Courtney	Cecil	m	50	6	6	6	4	5	4	4	3	4	4
Harriet	George	m	57	5	5	4	4	4	4	3	4	4	4
McIntyre	Jack	m	52	4	4	4	4	5	4	4	3	3	5
Minor	Maurice	m	25	3	2	2	3	4	3	2	3	4	4
Moon	James	m	56	6	6	6	5	6	4	6	3	3	6
York	Evans	m	49	6	6	6	6	6	5	5	3	4	4

Look at the two versions of the database for Class 7 above. The first version lists all 20 pupils in alphabetical order. The second version lists the girls first and then the boys. Each group is in alphabetical order.

C1 Here are some printouts from the Class 7 database. Work out the rule Miss Reed used to get each one. Which would be a good list to be on? Which would be a bad one.

Printout 1

surname	first name	gender	attendance	Eng	math	sci	tech	hist	geog	French	art	music	PE
Minor	Maurice	m	25	3	2	2	3	4	3	2	3	4	4
Knowles	Jennifer	f	27	3	3	3	3	4	6	4	4	2	3
Bentall	Felicity	f	45	4	4	5	5	3	4	4	4	4	4
English	Norma	f	47	7	6	6	5	5	5	5	3	4	4
Byfleet	Shuman	m	47	4	4	4	4	5	4	5	3	2	4
Hassan	Eliza	f	48	5	5	5	6	5	5	4	3	3	4
York	Evans	m	49	6	6	6	6	6	5	5	3	4	4

Printout 2

surname	first name	gender	attendance	English	maths	science
Courtney	Cecil	m	50	6	6	6
English	Norma	f	47	7	6	6
German	Angela	f	50	7	7	6
Kassel	Honey	f	59	7	7	7
Moon	James	m	56	6	6	6
Orion	Frances	f	58	6	7	6
Pendang	Phui	f	55	5	6	5
York	Evans	m	49	6	6	6

Printout 3

surname	first name	gender	attendance	English	maths	science
Courtney	Cecil	m	50	6	6	6
English	Norma	f	47	7	6	6
German	Angela	f	50	7	7	6
Kassel	Honey	f	59	7	7	7
Moon	James	m	56	6	6	6
Orion	Frances	f	58	6	7	6
York	Evans	m	49	6	6	6

D Names and addresses

Name	Location	Continent	Major eruptions	Last
Awu	Indonesia	Asia	1711, 1856, 1892	1968
Bezymianny	USSR	Asia	1955–6	1984
Cosequina	Nicaragua	S America	1835	1835
El Chichon	Mexico	S America	1982	1982
Erebus	Antarctica	Antarctica	1947, 1972	1986

The database on page 43 has 38 **records**, one for each volcano.

It has five **fields** as follows:

Name Location Continent Major eruptions Last

surname	first name	gender	attendance	Eng	math	sci	tech	hist	geog	French	art	music	PE
Bentall	Felicity	f	45	4	4	5	5	3	4	4	4	4	4
Bordon	Alan	m	55	4	4	4	3	4	4	4	3	4	4
Byfleet	Shuman	m	47	4	4	4	4	5	4	5	3	2	4
Courtney	Cecil	m	50	6	6	6	4	5	4	4	3	4	4
English	Norma	f	47	7	6	6	5	5	5	5	3	4	4
German	Angela	f	50	7	7	6	7	6	4	4	3	4	4
Harriet	George	m	57	5	5	4	4	4	4	3	4	4	4

The class database on page 45 has 20 records, one for each pupil. It has the following 14 fields:

Surname
First name
Gender
Attendance
English
Maths
Science
Technology
History
Geography
French
Art
Music
PE

Notice that some of the field names were shortened in some printouts.

Here is a computer record displayed on a screen. It is taken from a database which holds names, addresses and telephone numbers.

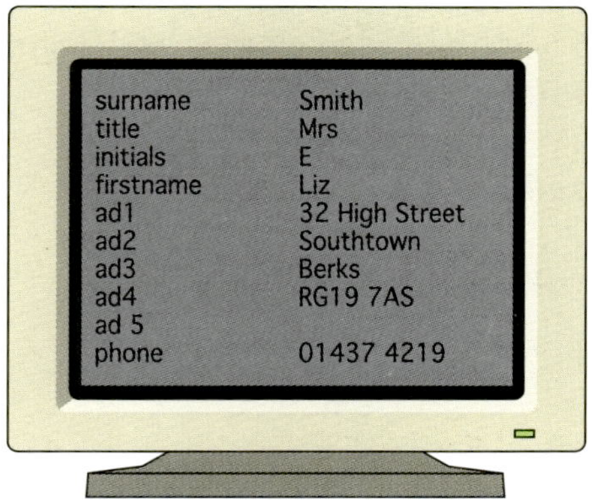

The database contains over 1000 records. It uses the following ten fields:

Surname	ad2
title	ad3
initials	ad4
firstname	ad5
ad1	phone

(Note: ad1 stands for the first line of the address, ad2 the second, and so on.)

D1 Which fields are used in this address label?

D2 Which fields are used in a telephone directory?

Smith, Ms E (Liz) 01437 4219
Smith, Mr F (Fred) 0171 428 9271
Smith, Mr R (Roger)............0121 324 0047

Before you use a database you must decide what fields you will need when you enter your data.

E A simple spreadsheet

On page 1 Mohammed, James and Tonia collected some data about sports.

They asked 28 pupils all from class 7J.

Their results were:

Football	8
Cricket	6
Swimming	3
Horse racing	1
Hockey	3
Tennis	7

Next day they asked the 29 pupils in class 7K the same question and their results were:

Football	12
Cricket	2
Swimming	5
Horse racing	0
Hockey	2
Tennis	8

They now have two sets of data which they could put on cards as in Section A. Each card would have a title, 7J or 7K, to tell them apart.

But it might be simpler to put all the data on the same sheet. A sheet like this is called a **spreadsheet**:

	7J	7K	
Football	8	12	
Cricket	6	2	
Swimming	3	5	
Horse racing	1	0	
Hockey	3	2	
Tennis	7	8	

E1 Write down some advantages of writing data on a spreadsheet.

Mohammed, James and Tonia continued to ask the same question and their results were:

	7J	7K	7L	7M	Total
Football	8	12	7	9	
Cricket	6	2	5	5	
Swimming	3	5	4	6	
Horse racing	1	0	0	0	
Hockey	3	2	5	6	
Tennis	7	8	10	4	

E2 Copy and complete this table by filling in the final column.

E3 What sport is the most popular with all 118 pupils?

E4 Present the information given in the Total column as a bar graph like this (one bar has been put in to help you):

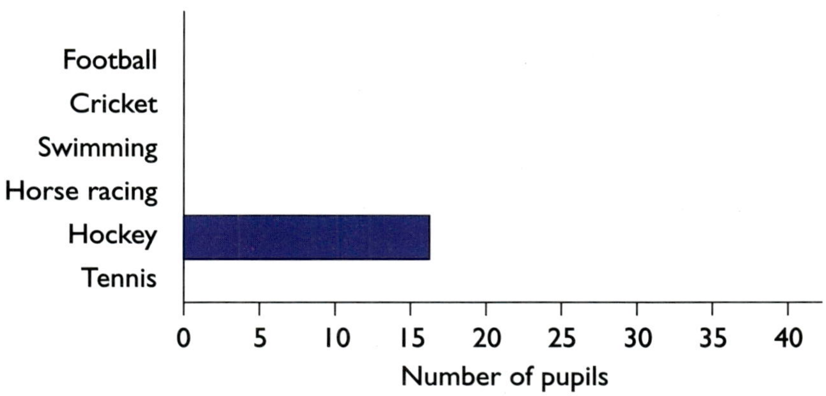

E5 Write down the sports in descending order of popularity. (Start with the most popular one.)

UNIT 6 Using averages

A Revision

You should remember from Unit 2 that there are three kinds of average.

They are:

The mean – is what you get when all the values are made equal.

The median – is the middle value when all the values are listed in order of size.

The mode – is the commonest or most frequent value.

When people talk about average, they normally think of the mean or the **arithmetic mean**. This is calculated by adding up the value of all the items and dividing by the number of items.

The mean is only useful in some situations. In the following sections you will learn to decide which 'average' is best in different situations.

B The words on the pack

Questions **B1** to **B8** show some products and their labels that you may see at home and in shops.

For each product, write down what you think the words on the label mean. Also write down the highest and lowest values that you think are possible if the label is truthful.

B1

Average contents
48 matches

B2

Light bulb
average life
1000 hours

B3

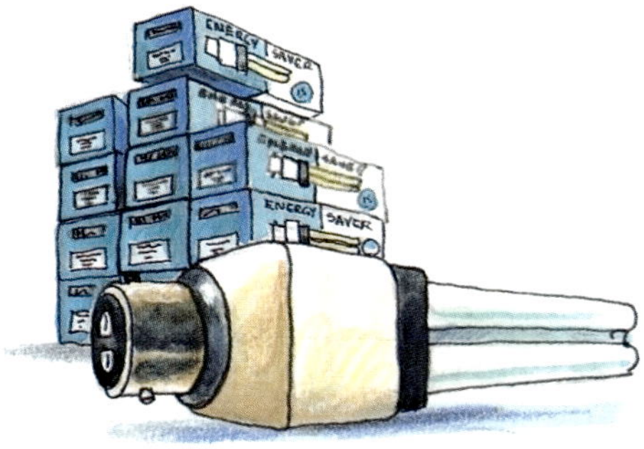

Energy saver bulb
average life
8000 hours

B4

Kitchen paper towels
average 70 sheets
per roll

B5

Breakfast cereal
This pack contains
approximately
10 servings

B6

Brilliant White Paint
On smooth surfaces the contents of this can will cover approximately
9 square metres

B7

Runner Beans
average seed content 50

B8

This jigsaw puzzle
contains approximately
300 pieces

B9 Find two more examples, similar to those in questions B1 to B8. Write down what you think the words on the label mean.

C Which average?

C1 The weights of nine pupils, measured in kilograms, are:

35, 55, 38, 61, 43, 47, 44, 37, 36

a Put the weights in order of size starting with the lightest.

b Find the median weight.

c Find the mean weight.

d Draw a graph, like the one below, to show the weights from the smallest (on the left) to the largest (on the right).
Colour the median weight in a different colour.
Draw a line across the graph to show the mean weight.

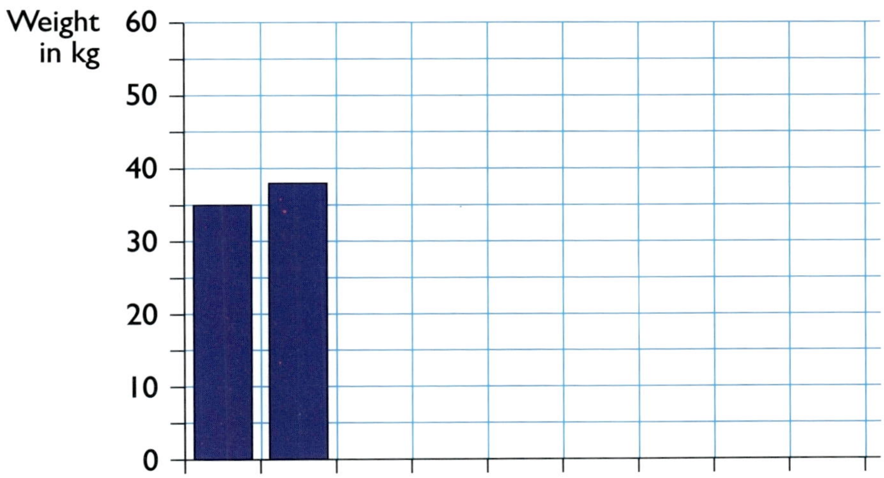

Both the median and mean weights have some meaning in question **C1**, but the mode does not make sense since no weight is repeated.

C2 The numbers of goals scored by a school football team in 15 games are:

0, 1, 0, 2, 0, 0, 1, 1, 0, 1, 0, 0, 1, 0, 1

Which 'average' describes the number of goals best?

Explain why the mean is not much use here.

C3 A packet containing four long-life batteries states:

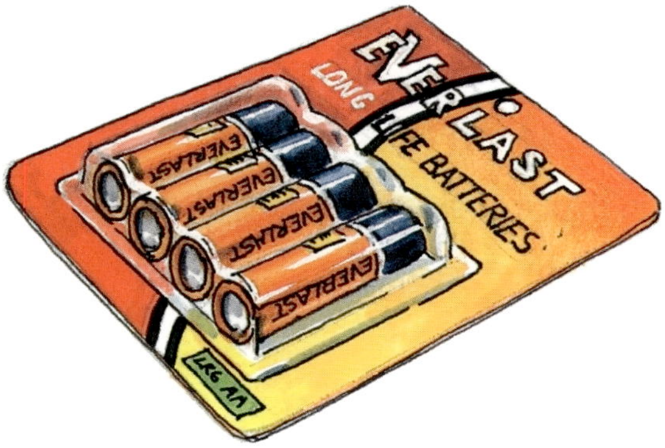

'last up to six times longer than ordinary zinc-carbon batteries'

What does this mean?

D Party time

D1 Suppose that you are planning a party for ten young children.

You know that their favourites are crisps, sausages, chocolate biscuits and cola drinks.

Write down what you think an 'average child' will eat and drink and use it to work out a shopping list for the party.

How would you make sure that there was enough variety for everyone?

E Rolling dice

E1 On page 3 you were given the results that two pupils got when they rolled two dice 100 times and recorded the total number of dots.

Here are their results again:

6	11	9	5	5	12	6	12	8	3
8	8	5	9	10	4	7	7	8	4
7	7	10	9	7	5	8	6	7	12
7	4	8	5	8	5	10	9	7	9
7	9	6	7	5	2	9	4	8	7
6	5	6	9	6	3	9	9	10	6
7	5	2	4	11	7	4	3	6	9
4	3	8	5	8	12	7	7	3	6
9	6	6	10	7	10	6	7	6	7
7	2	6	5	11	6	9	6	7	9

Find the mode.

If you turned back to page 3 you will have seen instantly, from the frequency table below the results, that the mode for question **E1** is 7.

E2 Is the mode *always* 7 when you roll two dice and add up the dots?

How would you find out?

If you did a practical experiment would you need as many as 100 throws to be sure of your answer?

If you roll a single dice and record the numbers, you know that all six numbers are equally likely. So you would expect each of the numbers to appear roughly the same number of times. It would not make sense to find the mode for throwing a single dice.

Extension work

3 dice

E3 Roll three dice a number of times and record the total number of dots each time. The lowest number you can obtain is 3 and the highest is 18. If you roll enough times, the mode should be either 10 or 11. Can you explain why there are two possible values?

F Experiments

In section B, you looked at labels on products.
How do you think the manufacturers decided what to write on the labels?
Did they guess how many matches are in a box or how many servings you can get from a packet of cereals?
Or did they do some experiments or count the pieces?

F1 Look at questions **B1** to **B8** again and decide in each case how you think the manufacturer worked out what to put on the label.

Not all your answers to question **F1** should be the same. Some of the labels can be decided by measuring or counting, but others will need to be decided by experiment.

F2 Choose one of the answers to question **F1** that must be decided by an experiment.

a Describe how you would do the experiment if you had enough time and money.

b If you repeated the experiment, would you expect to get exactly the same answer?

F3 Ten people are asked to estimate and mark on a strip of paper a length of 10 centimetres.

When measured to the nearest millimetre, the lengths they mark are:

7.9, 10.7, 9.8, 12.2, 11.7, 9.3, 10.4, 9.5, 10.3 and 9.2 cm

All the marks are then put on a single strip of paper:

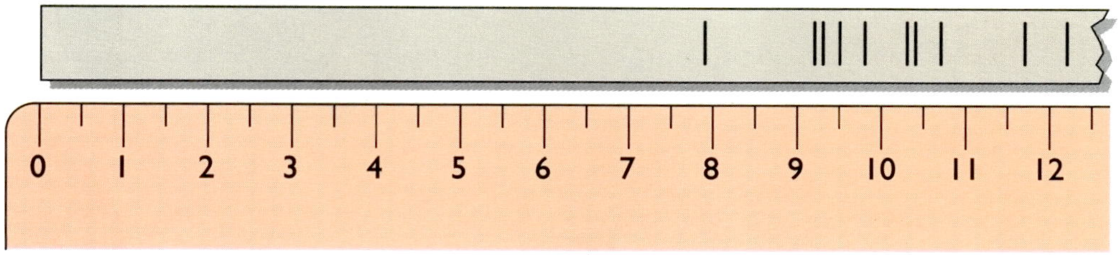

By looking at the marks, but without marking the paper, make an estimate of the mean value of the lengths.

Did you choose a value that had five marks on each side?

Is it always true that the mean value of the ten marks will have five marks on each side?

F4 Suppose you decide to set up a shop to sell sweets to your own class.

How would you start?

Here are some important factors that you might consider:

- type of sweet
- flavour
- cost
- size of packet

For each of these factors, you need to know what the 'average' pupil would wish to buy.

Choose one of these factors and decide what to stock in the shop.

G Finding averages

It is often useful to know what is an average value for something. Here are some everyday examples. In each case, try to decide what is an average or typical value.

G1 The cost of a can of cola drink

What is the average price of a can?

Does it matter if the cans are different brands or sizes?

a Find about ten different prices.

b Write down what you think is the most typical price.

G2 Time taken travelling to school

a Does it make sense to give an average time for pupils in your class? Why?

b Is it sensible to mix up pupils who travel by different methods?

c What do you do if one pupil is *much* different from the average?

d Who would be interested to know about your average travelling time?

G3 How fast do you think you can move?

How long does it take you to cover 100 metres?

What is a typical time for

- walking
- running
- hopping?

Would a typical time for 200 metres be double the previous answers?

G4 How long is a queue?

Do people only wait in queues if there is no alternative or if they really want something such as a bus home?

Do you go to another shop if there is a queue at the first shop?

Think of different situations where there are queues and work out: how many people are waiting in a typical queue?

UNIT 7 Using data

A Broken down by age

Here are figures for the population of the United Kingdom, broken down by age:

Age	Thousands
0–9	7440.4
10–19	7463.5
20–29	9269.4
30–39	7766.7
40–49	7374.4
50–59	6057.9
60–69	5867.5
70–79	3935.1
over 80	2061.5

Source: Guinness UK Data Book

It may be easier to write the numbers in millions:

Age	Millions
0–9	7.4
10–19	7.5
20–29	

A1 Copy and complete the table above.

Then show the data in a bar graph.

The bars can go horizontally or vertically, as you please.

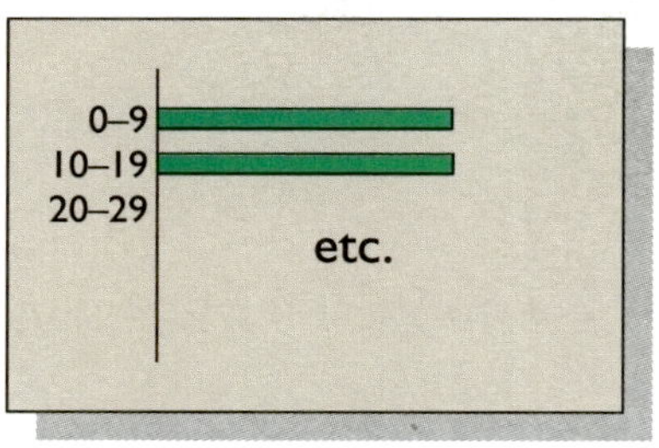

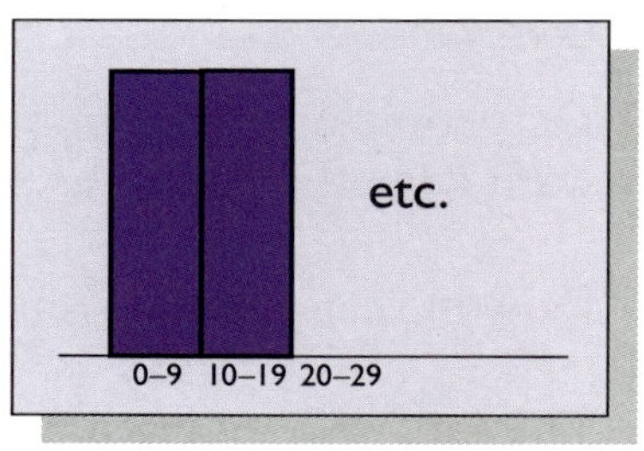

A2 Here are figures for the ages of people living on the fictitious island of Min.

15	32	50	79	36	46	60	80	49	50	42	33	66	31	61	5	46	42	3	1
61	37	62	14	24	18	27	55	46	30	14	45	65	8	59	38	32	8	20	60
34	69	13	52	33	57	10	25	15	2	25	29	25	16	65	13	51	74	47	40
3	42	53	13	15	68	55	24	50	76	33	51	33	33	5	23	80	64	15	15
73	8	29	71	60	49	37	30	32	12	75	37	53	44	73	16	48	6	19	57
3	35	37	62	4	20	52	63	43	43	3	16	26	42	42	5	42	73	69	64

a Make a bar graph for this data.

b Are the ages of people on Min distributed in the same way as the ages of people in the UK as a whole?

Here is a graph that claims to show the breakdown by age of the population of Australia, but there is something wrong with it.

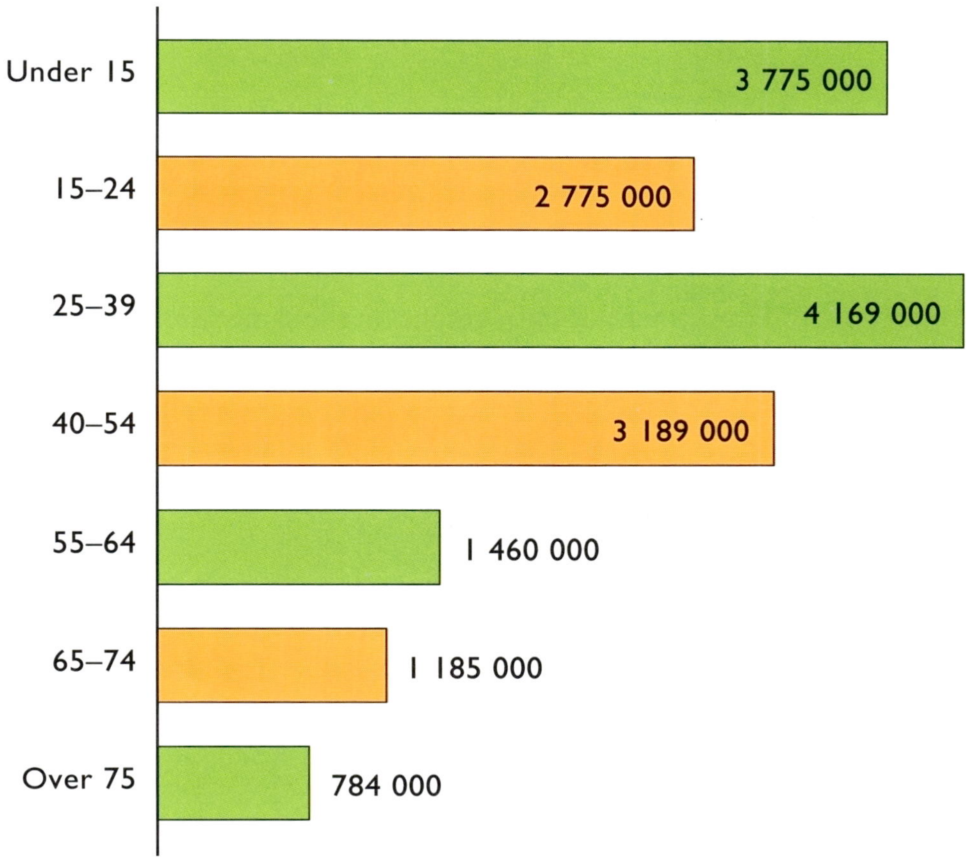

The ages are not grouped equally.

You cannot make a bar graph with equal groups from these figures.

B House prices

Here are some figures on average house prices in Britain:

	New houses (£)	All houses (£)
1966	3910	3850
1970	4990	5000
1975	12234	11945
1980	26131	23514
1982	27914	24577
1984	33416	29648
1986	42319	36869
1988	61551	52632
1990	75403	64657
1991	75065	65904

Source: Guinness UK Data Book

B1 Show this information in line graphs.

You can either put both graphs on the same sheet or draw two separate graphs.

B2 Write a few sentences about the graphs.

Survey of local house prices

newspapers

B3 Find out, for example by studying house advertisements in your local paper, whether house prices in your area are similar to those in the table.

Write your conclusions in a short report, giving reasons for what you find.

C Words, words, words

newspapers, books

C1 Investigate the lengths of words used in two different newspapers or books by different authors.

a Show your results using suitable graphs.

b Is it sensible to work out average word lengths?

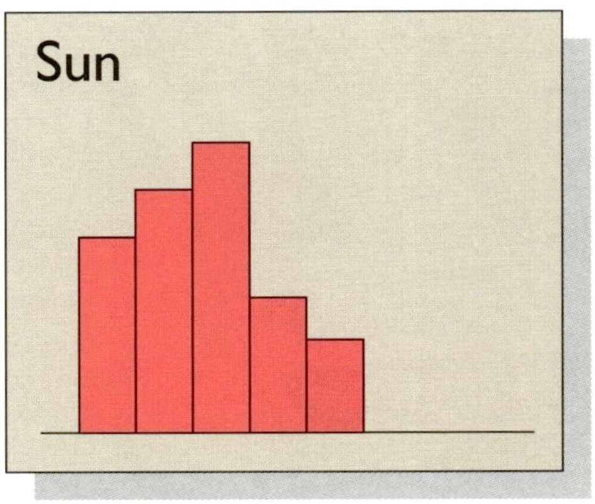

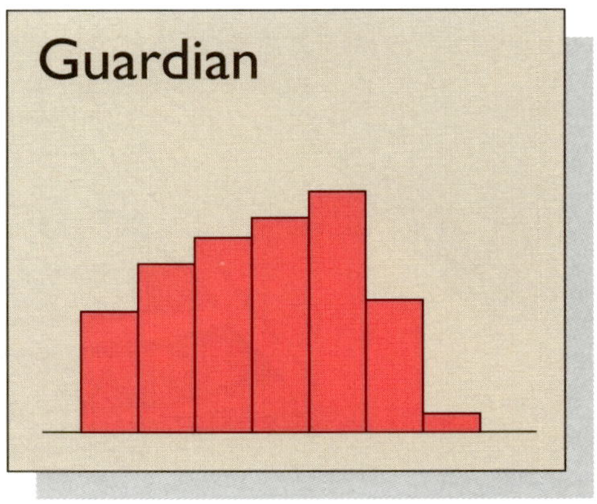

If you like, you can use the two extracts opposite, but it is probably better to choose your own samples.

C2 Investigate other factors such as length of sentences and length of articles.

Road pricing gears up

Rebecca Smithers
Transport Correspondent

THE Government will take its first formal step this week towards road pricing as a means of easing congestion in city centres when it sets out options for the technology.

It plans to publish the extensive research programme on technology, leaving the wider issues, including costs, until later.

The paper, expected to be published by the Department of Transport on Wednesday, will refer to "city congestion charging" because ministers believe this a politically more acceptable description.

The first part will set out the practicalities of pre-paid cards and of monitoring drivers with roadside equipment.

Officials have been examining foreign schemes such as those in Norway and Sweden.

Sources say components of the study include: whether road pricing is acceptable, how the revenue would be used (whether it would be diverted to other transport projects), and its impact on traffic patterns.

The Government is keen to get a pilot study under way, and one of the first schemes is being put in place in Cambridge.

Motorists will have to acquire a pre-paid windscreen display card, which can be checked by equipment being installed this summer.'

The Department of Transport is also looking at whether people would stagger their work hours in response to peak-hour pricing in London.

A separate green paper after Easter will examine the use of tolls on inter-urban roads and concentrate on options for introducing charges on new motorways and trunk roads and on those which have been widened and improved.

● Motorists could be charged for using existing motorways as a means of improving and widening existing roads, the Transport Secretary, John MacGregor, warned yesterday on BBC's Money Programme.

Source: The *Guardian*

Cops take on ravers

POLICE will be handed sweeping powers this week to crack down on ravers and hippies.

Home Secretary Kenneth Clarke will enable them to turn cars away from raves, seize DJs equipment and ban convoys of more than six hippie vehicles.

A new law of "aggravated trespass" will allow police to arrest offenders who abuse farmers or damage their property.

'Flood' of refugees

FOREIGN Secretary Douglas Hurd yesterday warned that Europe could be hit by a "tidal wave" of immigrants from former Soviet states.

He said millions will leave to find work in the West unless the EC helps Russian president Boris Yeltzin revive his economy.

Mr Hurd warned: "If we do not take action, a tidal wave could drench Europe."

Fears for aid Brits

FEARS were growing for four British aid workers last night after their convoy vanished in war-torn Bosnia.

Magistrate Bill Croaker, 56, and three helpers left the Croatian port of Split last week to take aid to Tuzla.

The four members of the Bosnia Aid committee of Oxford were due back six days ago.

Officials fear the convoy may have been hijacked by Serb bandits.

Source: The *Sun*

D Population explosion

D1 Here are some figures for the population of the United Kingdom over the last two hundred years or so:

Year	Population (millions)
1801	12
1821	15
1841	20
1861	24
1881	30
1901	38
1921	43
1941	48
1961	52
1981	56

Source: Guinness UK Data Book

a Show these figures on a line graph.

b Write a few sentences about the data.

c Does the graph surprise you?

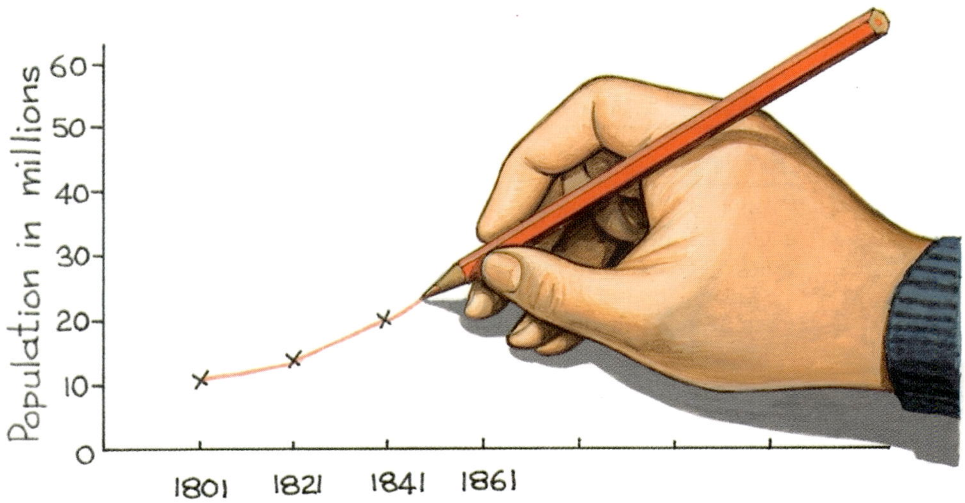

D2 Use your graph to estimate the population in

a 2001

b 3001

Extension work

D3 If Magic Fish Feed is given to the fish in a pond every day, the number of fish in the pond will be *one and a half times* what it was the day before.

Make a table to show how the population grows.

D4 Do you think this example of growth is at all realistic?

E Your own survey

E1 You are going to conduct a survey on a topic of your own choice. You may prefer to work with a partner or in small groups.

You should go through the following steps:

1. Decide what you could do with the information you collect, or what question it might help to answer.
2. Decide exactly what question or questions you are going to ask.
3. Carry out the survey.
4. Write your report.
5 Finally, think whether you achieved what you intended. What improvements might you make if you did it again?

If you like, you can use the headings of the form opposite.

Instead of *doing* a survey, you may be able to write about one that you have done already.

Survey on
by
Date
The problems
We wanted information that would help
with this problem:
The questions
The actual questions we asked were:
The findings

UNIT 8 *Possible choices*

A The Basketball League

A1 There are four teams in the Basketball League. They play on Saturday afternoons. Each team plays every other team twice, once at home and once away.

a Draw up a fixture list.

b If possible, compare your fixture list with other people's list.

A2 Suppose that there are only three teams.

a Make a fixture list.

b Say what you think about it.

More teams want to join the league.

A3 Make a list for six teams.

A4 Make a list for five teams.

Extension work

A5 Investigate lists for more than six teams.

B Happy families

B1 Susan dreams of having a family of three children. She could have a boy, then a girl, then another boy. Or she could have a girl, then another girl, then a boy. Or she could have …

Make a list of all the possibilities.

Susan could have	boy, boy, boy
	boy, boy, girl
	girl,

(There should be eight of them.)

B2 Susan would really like three girls.

If she has three children, is it likely they will all be girls?

B3 If she has three children, what is the chance that they will all be girls?

C Take a seat

C1 Alan, Barbara, Cathy and David are to sit on four chairs.

List *all* the ways this can be done, using the first letter of their name. If you find this too complicated, try three people only.

C2 **a** How many possible ways did you find for A, B, C and D to sit?

b How many of these had A and B sitting next to each other?

D Telephone numbers

D1 A telephone number contains the digits 2, 3 and 9, but Philip cannot remember the order.

How many different numbers can be made using these three digits? List them all.

> It could be 239
> or 293
> or

D2 Philip decides to try each number until he gets the right one. Here are some possibilities:

A He gets the right number first time

B He gets it right sooner or later

C He gets it inside three tries

D He gets it in two tries

a Arrange these possibilities in order of likelihood

b Mark them on a probability line. Where possible, give the chances for each.

c Think of some more possibilities and add them to your list.

impossible — certain

D3 **a** If each telephone call costs 10 pence, how much must Philip be prepared to spend?

b How much do you think he is likely to spend?

D4 What do you think what could go wrong with his plan?

D5 Suppose that the unknown part of the telephone number has four digits, or five digits or more.

a Work out the number of possibilities in these cases.

b Work out the largest amount of money that Philip might have to spend.

E Decision trees

E1 Look at this picture and the **decision tree-diagram** below.

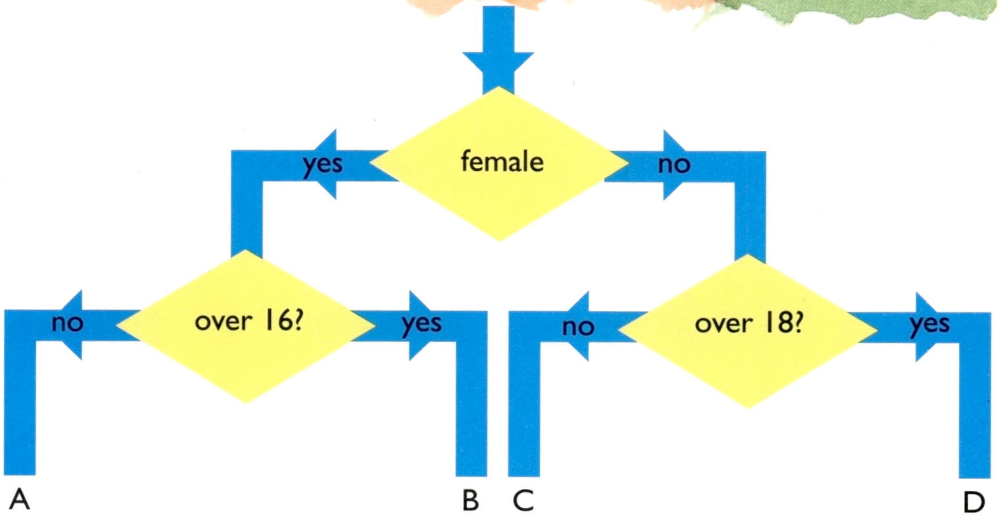

You should be able to see that John, aged 14, goes through Gate C and Mary, aged 20, goes through gate B.

Describe in words which people will enter by gate A. Which will enter by gate B? Which by each of the other gates?

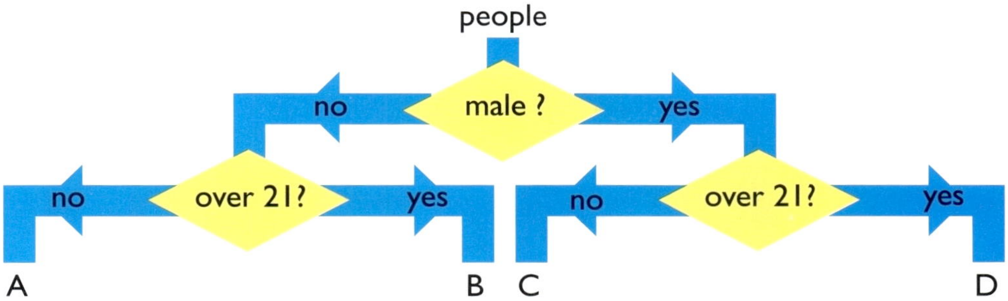

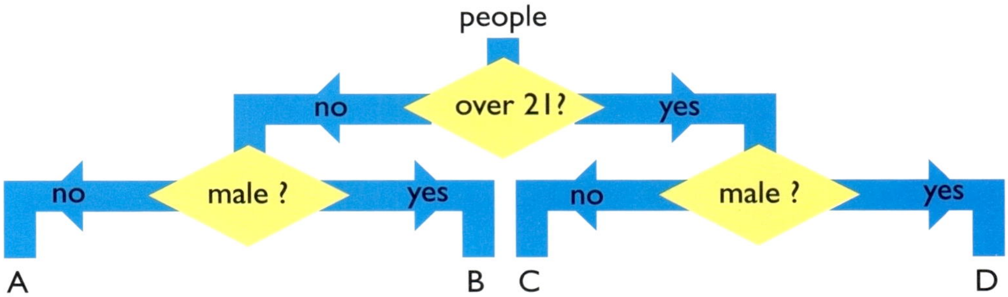

E2 **a** Do the same for these decision tree-diagrams.

b Are these two diagrams the same? If not, describe the differences.

E3 Make up decision tree-diagrams for some more situations.
In each case, describe clearly which people go through each of the gates.
You can have more than four gates if you want to.

F Odd numbers to the left

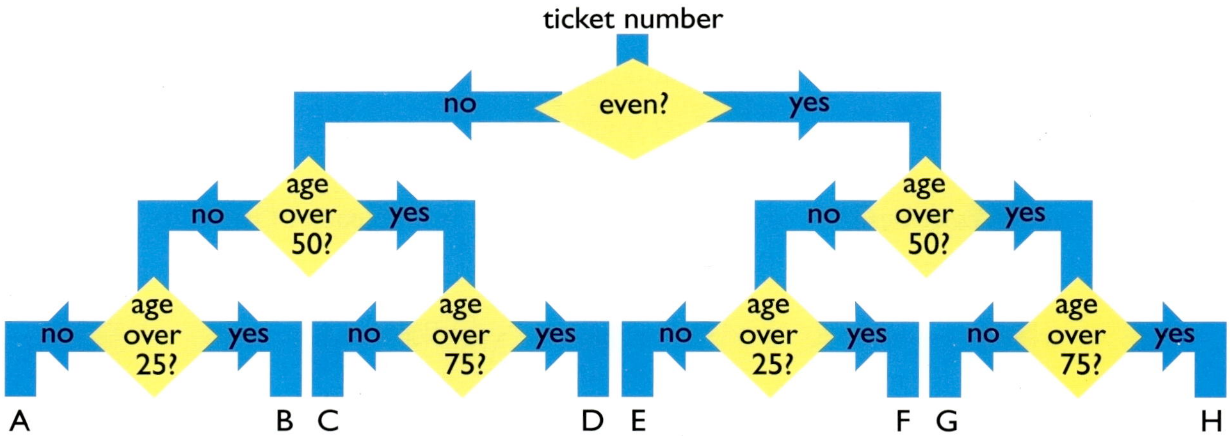

Use the decision tree-diagram to check that Jane, aged 16 with ticket number 25, will go through gate A.

F1 Through which gate will the following people go?

a Lesley, aged 30, with ticket number 71

b Martha, aged 77, with ticket number 102

c Norman, aged 53, with ticket number 13

d Otto, aged 13, with ticket number 60

F2 Describe in words the people who will go through

a gate C **b** gate G.

F3 Make up some more decision tree-diagrams for sorting numbers. In each case, describe the different categories that your diagram sorts the numbers into.

F4 Find the decision tree-diagrams that will sort numbers like this:

a 6, 12, 18 …

b 3, 9, 15, 21 …

c 2, 4, 8, 10, 14, 16 …

d 1, 5, 7, 11, 13 …

UNIT 9 Projects

In this Unit there are five projects. Look through them and choose the one you find most interesting. You may decide, after talking to your teacher, to carry out a similar project of your own choice. Some projects will take a lot of thought and time. Present your work so that it is clear to someone who knows very little about the topic.

A Holidays in the sun

Suppose that you wish to plan a family holiday for two adults and two children in the sunny islands of the Mediterranean Sea in August.

You will need to look at data on:

- the choice of resort
- the weather
- the cost
- the time of flights
- facilities available.

You can find useful information in holiday brochures from a travel agent. But you may find it easier to use the simplified information given here for three imaginary resorts: Cayley, Newton and Venn.

	Cayley	Newton	Venn
Daily maximum temperature in °C	27	30	28
Daily hours of sunshine	11	11	10
London Daily maximum temperature 22 Daily hours of sunshine 6			

Facility	Cayley	Newton	Venn
Beaches	crowded sunbathing watersports	clean white sand with a gentle slope	numerous uncrowded beaches
Shopping	good for porcelain novelties, leather goods	good for pearls, leather, jewellery	good for shoes, T-shirts, handicrafts
Excursions	plenty of tours to places of interest	several tours available	no tours available
Sport	waterskiing sailing parascending squash horse-riding golf	tennis windsurfing	tennis golf windsurfing sailing

Cost of accommodation for 2 adults and 2 children for 14 days

	Cayley	Newton	Venn
Apartments self-catering	£700	£900	£1400
Hotel half-board	£950	£1200	£1600
Better hotel full-board	£1100	£1350	not available

A1 Write down your proposed holiday and give reasons for your choice.

B Planning a weekend

After a busy week at school, you want to plan a pleasant weekend.

Make a plan for a weekend, including some homework and a Saturday job or jobs in the house if these are part of what you do normally.

You might include:

- shopping
- a party
- watching or playing a game
- playing records
- making music
- watching television.

Your reasons for choosing an activity might include:

- time taken
- cost
- want to meet people
- want to be quiet
- need to buy clothes.

Make a table of some of the possible choices and list the advantages and disadvantages.

Your table could look like this:

Activity	**Average time taken**	**Advantages**	**Disadvantages**
Shopping			
A party			
Watching or playing a game			
Playing records			
Making music			
Watching television			

Make a rough timetable of what you decide to do, with the reasons for your choice like this:

Time	**Activity**	**Reasons**
Friday evening		
Saturday morning		
Saturday afternoon		
Saturday evening		
Sunday morning		
Sunday afternoon		
Sunday evening		

C A day out

Suppose your class is asked to plan an educational day out from school. You could use real data and plan for a real trip.

If this is not possible, here are some ideas for an imaginary trip. You are at the school in Aytown in the middle of the map.

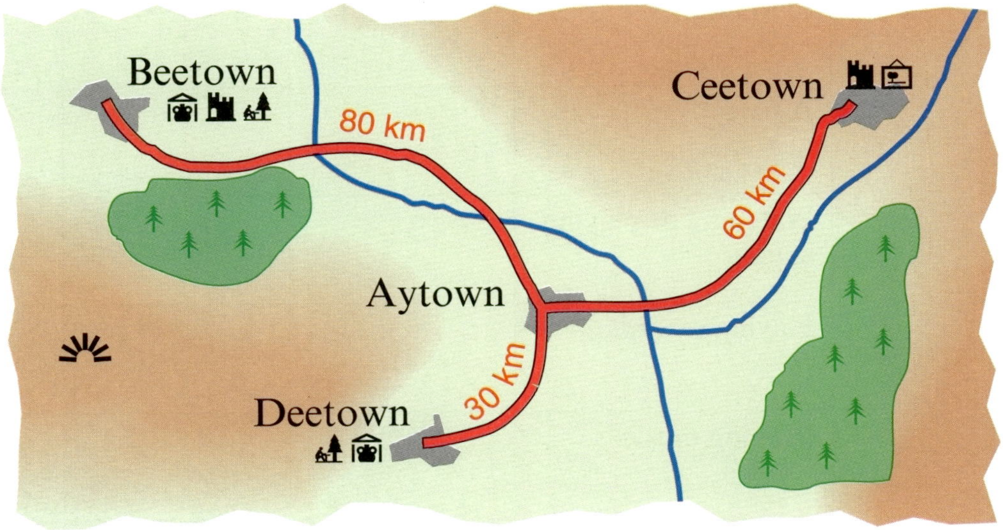

It is summer and the weather is expected to be good, but it could rain.

There are three possible places of interest:

	Museum	Park	Art gallery	Castle
Beetown	✔	✔		✔
Ceetown			✔	✔
Deetown	✔	✔		

The cost of a coach is £50 a day plus £1 for each kilometre travelled. A coach can carry 45 people.

The admission costs are:

Museums	£1.50	each pupil
Castles	£2.00	each pupil
Art gallery	free	
Parks	free	

The opening hours are:

Museums	10:00 a.m. to 4:30 p.m.
Castles	9:30 a.m. to 7:30 p.m.
Art gallery	11:00 a.m. to 5:30 p.m.
Parks	8:00 a.m. to 8:00 p.m.

You will also need to know that the museums and art gallery are closed on Monday.

You will need to decide:

- the timetable for the day
- the cost per pupil assuming 30 pupils go
- the arrangements for drinks or meals.

Discuss alternative plans for the day, showing costs and giving reasons for your final choice.

D What to watch on television

This project is about planning a sequence of television programmes for a Saturday evening's viewing from 6:00 p.m. to 9:00 p.m.

An imaginary list of programmes is given below.

You may prefer to use a current edition of the *Radio Times* or *TV Times* or a similar list of programmes.

<table>
<tr><th></th><th>BBC1</th><th>BBC 2</th><th>ITV</th><th>Channel 4</th><th>Sky Movies</th><th>Sky Sports</th></tr>
<tr><td>6:00–6:30</td><td>News</td><td rowspan="3">Rugby football</td><td rowspan="2">Drama series</td><td>Soap opera</td><td rowspan="4">Showcase</td><td rowspan="4">Horse racing</td></tr>
<tr><td>6:30–7:00</td><td>Jo will fix it</td><td>Viewer's comments</td></tr>
<tr><td>7:00–7:30</td><td>Superman</td><td>Star guest</td><td rowspan="2">Politics</td></tr>
<tr><td>7:30–8:00</td><td>Comedy show</td><td>News and sport</td><td>Comedy show</td></tr>
<tr><td>8:00–8:30</td><td>Real life</td><td rowspan="2">Documentary film</td><td>Home videos</td><td rowspan="2">Film about animals</td><td rowspan="2">Film (until 10:00)</td><td rowspan="2">Football</td></tr>
<tr><td>8:30–9:00</td><td>News & sport</td><td>News</td></tr>
</table>

Your reasons for choosing programmes might include:

- It's a good series
- I don't like politics
- I only watch sport
- I don't enjoy serious programmes.

Make a table like the one below.

Choose your own times if you prefer.

	Programme chosen	Reasons for choice
6:00 – 6:30		
6:30 – 7:00		
7:00 – 7:30		
7:30 – 8:00		
8:00 – 8:30		
8:30 – 9:00		

You may think that this exercise is unrealistic because people do not plan watching television in this way. They do other things at the same time and other people are involved in the choice.

Write down some reasons in favour of planning an evening's viewing like this and some reasons against. Can you suggest a better way of planning?

E Buying clothes

Imagine that you have a present of £75 with which to buy clothes.

You decide that, if possible, you would like to buy some jeans, a T-shirt and a pair of shoes.

You decide that you will look for the following:

- a good fit (or will I grow soon?)
- a suitable colour and design
- the right price
- good wearing quality
- warmth.

Does it matter what you buy first?

Will you look at several shops before you buy?

What questions will you ask the shop assistant?

If possible, find out some details of your own.

Otherwise, use the following imaginary data:

	Good brand	**Cheaper brand**	**Unbranded**
Jeans	good range of styles and colours £30	limited range but good quality £20	hardwearing but not well made; no choice £10
T-shirt	variety of styles, colours and materials £12	well made but limited range £7	good value but only in thin white cotton £3
Shoes	good variety and quality £70	limited variety, good quality £35	poor quality, plenty of styles £15

Write down how you would make your choice.

Remember that the total cost must be less than £75.

Give reasons for each item that you decide to buy.

If you used the table above, what extra information would have been useful?

Handling data 1
National curriculum level description coverage

NC level and description	Covered in pupil's book unit:
• collect discrete data and record them using a frequency table	1
• understand and use the mode and median	2, 6
• group data, where appropriate, in equal class intervals, represent collected data in frequency diagrams and interpret such diagrams	4, 7
• construct and interpret simple line graphs	4, 7
• understand and use simple vocabulary associated with probability, including 'fair', 'certain', and 'likely'	3, 8
• using and applying the above skills	All units, but especially 5, 9